A Walk on the Wild Side
Walking with the Master

Dave Ens

Winnipeg, MB   Hillsboro KS

A Walk on the Wild Side

Copyright © 1998 by Kindred Productions, Winnipeg, Manitoba, Canada

All rights reserved. With the exception of brief excerpts for reviews, no part of this book may be reproduced, stored in a retrieval system or transmitted in whole or in part, in any form by any means, electronic, mechanical, photocopying, recording or otherwise without written permission of Kindred Productions.

Published simultaneously by Kindred Productions, Winnipeg, Manitoba R2L 2E5 and
Kindred Productions, Hillsboro, Kansas 67063

All scripture quotations, unless otherwise indicated, are taken from the HOLY BIBLE NEW INTERNATIONAL VERSION®. NIV®. Copyright © 1973, 1978, 1984 by International Bible Society. Used by permission of Zondervan Publishing House. All rights reserved. Other versions used include: the New Revised Standard Version of the Bible [NRSV], copyright 1989 by the Division of Christian Education of the National Council of the Churches of Christ in the USA; the THE MESSAGE [MES], copyright © by Eugene H.Peterson 1993, 1994, 1995, used by permission of NavPress Publishing Group; the New Living Translations [NLT], copyright © 1996, used by permission of Tyndale House Publishers, Inc. Wheaton Illinois 60189 ; and the Today's English Version [TEV], copyright © American Bible Society 1966, 1971, 1976.

This guide was written using "Mark" An Interpretation: A Bible Commentary for Teaching and Preaching by Lamar Williamson, Jr, 1983 as a reference.

Book Design: Makus Design, Winnipeg, Manitoba
Cover Design: Makus Design, Winnipeg, Manitoba

ISBN: 0-921788-56-8
Printed in Canada

Dear Young Person:

You are about to embark on a radical adventure with God. But let's get one thing straight right off the bat, if you're not looking for God and you want nothing to do with him, then this guide isn't for you. Just go ahead and close the book and don't read another word – I mean it.

If you have a desire to find out more about God, this guide will be helpful. Everything in here comes straight from the Bible. It's called *A Walk on the Wild Side* because the Bible actually is a pretty radical book. It's radical because it is words from God and when you read it, you realize that it asks you to do some wild stuff with your life.

Each day you'll read a passage, a key verse, and find a way to apply God's word to your life. There is space for journaling thoughts, ideas or questions for God.

Remember you need to start with a desire to know more about God and he will reveal himself to you. I pray that you will find him in a new way and learn more about living your life in his Word.

Dave Ens

Here's how it works. . .

The first thing you want to do is read the Scripture passage. This is the focus of the devotional! The other stuff is there to help explain it. It is all from the NIV unless indicated otherwise. *

Second, read through the section called **About the Passage**. This section will give you some background to what the passage is about. Sometimes, at the end of **The Application** you'll find some questions you can answer in the journal area. Or there might be an exercise for you to do throughout the week. Other times, there will not be any guidance given. Feel free to use the journal area for some thoughts of your own, for talking to God about your day or for writing down your prayers. That leads to the third thing...

Pray at the end. It doesn't have to be a long, profound prayer. Let it be a simple conversation with God, talking as you would to a friend. But it is important that you do pray. If you feel challenged by something you read, pray about that, or if a friend's name comes to mind, pray for that person, or if you want, just praise God for who he is.

If you make a decision to do something different in your life, talk to someone about it. It can be anyone you trust, a friend your age, your parents, your pastor, or a youth sponsor. They would love to talk to you about questions you have or decisions you want to make.

*(NIV) = New International Version, (NRSV) = New Revised Standard Version, (NLT) = New Living Translation, (TEV) = Today's English Version, (MES) = The Message

I Wanna Be Like Jesus

Scripture: Philippians 2:1-11

Key Verse: Each of you should look not only to your own interests, but also to the interests of others. Your attitude should be the same as that of Christ Jesus. *(Philippians 2:4-5)*

About the Passage

Take a minute and imagine what your life would be like if you had everything you ever wanted—not just money but things like friends, cars, popularity, etc. Pretty awesome to think about. Now, think about giving that all away to other people and ending up with nothing—not even a friend to talk to. The only reason you'd do it is because you knew that other people needed it. Would you do it?

Philippians 2 talks about being like Jesus by following his example in everyday life. It says that we need to have the same mind that Jesus had. Jesus is the one who had everything, nothing was lacking. He was in heaven—literally! But he gave it all up for you and me. That's pretty wild!

You see, Jesus knew that the only way we were going to get to heaven was for him to give it up. So he did. He came to earth and became a regular person. He laughed and cried and felt all the emotions that you feel—every single one of them. He also tried to tell us about the place he had given up. Some were offended and so they killed him.

But the wild thing is that dying was all part of the plan. In making the supreme sacrifice, Jesus gave the ultimate example of what God is all about. So even when Jesus died, God was glorified. The hard thing about this passage is that Paul (writer of Philippians) is saying that just as Jesus gave everything for other people, so should we.

A Walk on the Wild Side: Walking with the Master

The Application

Sometimes following Christ seems pretty overwhelming, doesn't it? It seems that there are so many things that you CAN'T do, so many rules you have to follow and so many restrictions. I know that in my own Christian life, there have been times when I have been frustrated with how wrong things seem to be going. It seems I can't do anything right. But the point of being a Christian isn't to keep track of all the things you do wrong. Christianity means being like Jesus. The whole idea is quite simple. In Phil. 2:3 it says, "Don't be selfish; don't live to make a good impression on others. Be humble, thinking of others as better than yourself." (NLT)

Putting others ahead of yourself takes some work. So here's a challenge for you. Make two columns in your journal, one saying "Opportunities" and the other, "Date." Then as you go through your day, keep track of all the times you can put others before yourself (whether or not you took advantage of it). Maybe it's as simple as opening the door for someone, or letting someone go ahead of you in the food line. I think you'll be surprised at the number of opportunities you have. In a selfish world, people who think of others first are rare and precious.

Remember the example of Christ, even in giving the ultimate sacrifice God was glorified. Maybe no one will say "thank you" or give you a pat on the back. They might even make fun of you, but God will be working through you and maybe that person will see God in you. Just think, because of your sacrifice, God will be glorified! That's a pretty wild thing to think about.

My thoughts to the Master

Starting the Journey

Scripture: Mark 1:1-15

Key Verse: After John was put in prison, Jesus went into Galilee, proclaiming the good news of God. "The time has come," he said. "The kingdom of God is near. Repent and believe the good news!" (Mark 1:14-15)

About the Passage

It's always a good thing to start at the beginning. That's why, as we walk with Jesus through the gospels, we start at Mark 1:1. Without the whole picture, you miss something. It's like trying to watch a two-hour movie starting an hour into it. You always find yourself asking, "Who's that guy," or "What are they looking for anyway?" It's also true of the Christian life. You have to start at the beginning.

It's neat to see how Jesus started at the beginning of his ministry. One of his first recorded acts as a human was to make a commitment to God through baptism. Only after that did he carry on with the task. Although there is a difference between the baptism of Jesus and "Believer's baptism," the public nature of the act says the same thing.

To understand this fully, you first need to know what baptism stands for. It is the "cleaning" of a person's life, the "washing" away of the old self and "raising up" the new. Through baptism, a person says publicly that, "I'm giving up my old way of living and I'm walking a new path!" You can also call it repentance. Jesus' baptism was a way for him to identify with the Father. Although the voice that calls down from heaven was only heard by Jesus (according to Mark), the act shows everyone that Jesus is on God's team!

Jesus' baptism also gives his preaching integrity. Imagine if you were in church on Sunday and heard some guy preach but you weren't sure if that person was a Christian. You probably wouldn't pay much attention to what was said. Likewise, Jesus' public act of identifying with God lets everyone know that he experienced what he's talking about and that he is on God's side.

The Application

I'm not sure where you're at in your Christian walk. Maybe you're just starting out or maybe you've been a Christian for as long as you can remember. But there is one thing you need to know—at some point in your walk, you're going to have to show whose side you're on. But that's a pretty tough thing to do, isn't it? It may mean that people look at you differently or even give you a hard time for it. But you need to understand that God doesn't want us to be "closet Christians." He doesn't want you to be a Christian on the "inside" and not on the "outside." That's why Jesus needed to be baptized. The voice told him that he was God's son but only he heard it. So he didn't just say, "Well, I know that I'm with God so that's good enough!" He showed everyone that he was with God.

If you're a Christian, do your friends know? If not, make a list of things that scare you about "declaring whose team you're on." Pray about those things, talk to God about them, talk to your parents, talk to someone you trust about them. There are no easy answers or solutions for this. You just have to take the step and do it. The good thing is that once people know who you are and what you stand for, it makes it a lot easier to talk to them about God.

If you've taken that step already, maybe baptism is an option for you. Maybe you're ready for that next step in your Christian walk. Again, pray about it, talk to someone about it. Know that God is taking these steps with you.

Things that scare me about "declaring whose team I'm on"

My thoughts to the Master

A Walk on the Wild Side: Walking with the Master

When He Calls – Go!

Scripture: Mark 1:16-22

Key Verse: Therefore, I urge you, brothers [& sisters], in view of God's mercy, to offer your bodies as living sacrifices, holy and pleasing to God—this is your spiritual act of worship. Do not conform any longer to the pattern of this world, but be transformed by the renewing of your mind. Then you will be able to test and approve what God's will is—his good, pleasing and perfect will. *(Romans 12:1-2)*

About the Passage

It doesn't take long to figure out what's remarkable about this passage (if you haven't, go back and look again). I am always blown away by the response Jesus gets to his commands. All he says is, "Come and follow me" and they do!! Simon (Peter) and Andrew leave their nets right where they are and follow him. James and John don't just leave their nets and their boat, but they leave their father sitting right there. Boy would I like to see the look on their dad's face! That is totally unbelievable.

This passage definitely says something about the authority of Jesus, doesn't it? Do you ever wonder what type of person Jesus was? I do. I wonder what type of person could call men and they would leave their jobs, their family, and their security just to follow him. And the really wild thing about this is that Jesus makes no promise to them about financial gain, job security, a good health plan, or even a nice house to live in. These men heard Jesus' call, followed him, and then looked at what the risks were.

The key is in the words they heard; or not so much the actual words but who was speaking. Those first disciples were lucky. They heard God's word right from God's mouth. Maybe they didn't know exactly who it was that was speaking, but they recognized those words to be authoritative. And so they listened and followed—just like that.

The Application

Don't you sometimes wish God would just rip open the heavens and shout down and let us all know exactly what's going on! I keep waiting for that "phone call" from God that will provide me with all the answers I need to solve my problems. But the fact is that he does speak to us—through the Bible. Just like audible words, the Bible is God's word and it speaks to us about many of the things we need to deal with. But more importantly, the Bible speaks to us about our relationship with God, through Jesus Christ. If we listen to God's word, we will hear it saying, "follow me!" The question is, what will you do when you hear it?

Do you think you could be like those first disciples who jumped up, left everything and followed Jesus? We tend to stop, sit down and think about the step we're about to take. We make charts weighing the "pros" and "cons" and consider all our options before we go ahead. We may even put a committee together to help us decide. There's something scary about giving up everything to follow Jesus, isn't there?

Remember the key verse in Philippians 2:4-5. We're so busy worrying about what will happen to us if we follow Jesus that we forget why we're doing it! Jesus' call to follow him is a call to a life of wild discipleship and this call demands an answer of all or nothing. What are the things that are stopping you from making a decision for Christ or from a bigger commitment? Write them down and take some time to pray about them.

A Walk on the Wild Side: Walking with the Master

My thoughts to the Master

The Basic Question of Faith

Scripture: Mark 1:21-34

Key Verse: If you confess with your mouth, "Jesus is Lord," and believe in your heart that God raised him from the dead, you will be saved. *(Romans 10:9)*

About the Passage

One of the very interesting things about the gospel of Mark is the fact that Jesus never wants anyone to say who he is. Scholars call it the "Messanic Secret" (pronounced mess-ee-an-ik). As we go through the book, you will see that many times this secret comes up. Yet it's only at the very end that it's revealed. Here we find the first case of that secret.

While Jesus is teaching in the synagogue, a demon possessed man enters. The demon recognizes Jesus right away, asking what "the Holy One of God" wants with him. Jesus tells him to be quiet and swiftly banishes him from the man he possessed. Everyone around is amazed and wonders what kind of power and authority it is that even the evil spirits obey him!

Do you see anything funny about that passage? If not, read it again (hey, it never hurts to read things twice). What I find very interesting, even funny, is the fact that evil spirits recognize Jesus right away and know who he is. All these people, on the other hand, are walking around, scratching their heads saying, "Who is this guy?" Jesus goes even further to show his authority by healing Simon's mother-in-law. By then, word got around and people started bringing Jesus all their sick, lame, and demon possessed. But still, no one knew who he was.

Here's an interesting thought. The demons know who Jesus is and know what he will do to them, so they scream and yell in anger and fear. The people have no clue who Jesus is but they flock to him because of what he can do for them. For the people, it doesn't matter who Jesus is. All that matters is that he can take care of their needs. Something to think about....

A Walk on the Wild Side: Walking with the Master

The Application

Have you ever seen one of those illustrations of Jesus that some people hang in their homes? You know the one where Jesus' perfect teeth are shining with an almost blinding radiance and his hair is thick and lustrous and perfectly in place. Many of us grew up with this image of Jesus in our minds. But regardless of the picture you have of what Jesus looks like, do you know who Jesus is?

Today's passage asks that basic question of faith. It's the most foundational question—do you know who Jesus is?

Is Jesus a "personal wish granter," or is he the one who looks after your needs (Matthew 6:25-34)? Is he there to make you happy, or is he there to walk with you in the most difficult times (Deut. 31:6)? Is he just a guy with some good ideas about life and stuff, or is he the "Holy One of God," the Son of the Most High (John 6:69)?

The reason this is so important is that if Jesus exists just so he can grant your wishes and satisfy your desires, then he really isn't a god at all, is he? Because then he is run by you! But if Jesus is the Christ, the Messiah, the Anointed One, the Son of God, then your relationship to him changes from self-centered to God-centered. So ask yourself if you recognize Jesus for who he really is. Do an inventory and check if your life is matching that. Take some time to pray and ask Jesus to open your heart and eyes to who he really is and what he wants to do in your life.

My thoughts to the Master

Keep Going By Stopping

Scripture: Mark 1:35-39

Key Verse: Give ear to my words, O LORD, consider my sighing. Listen to my cry for help, my King and my God, for to you I pray. In the morning, O LORD, you hear my voice; in the morning I lay my requests before you and wait in expectation. *(Psalm 5:1-3)*

About the Passage

I often wonder if Jesus ever felt proud of the work he had done. Think about it—here's a guy who can heal anything that is brought to him. He can cast out demons, get rid of someone's headache, and even make blind people see. Wouldn't you feel good about yourself after doing all that? However, the passage that you just read puts that all in perspective. Jesus knew what he was supposed to be doing here on earth. He also knew that the only way he was going to be able to keep going was to stop and take some time for himself and for God.

Take note that Mark doesn't just say "Jesus got up and went to pray." Instead, he makes a point of saying that it was very early in the morning, in fact, it was still dark out. So we're talking like 5 o'clock in the morning! Jesus gets up to go and pray. As we go through Mark, you'll find this event taking place other times (6:46 & 14:32). For Jesus, praying and time alone were very important disciplines he needed to get the job done.

Disciplines require some work and effort. They are things that help us grow as people and also grow in our relationship with God. Things like Bible reading, praying, fasting and celebrating in worship are all disciplines. So if you've got this far in this guide, you're on your way to having a regular discipline!

It seems to be that when times were the toughest, when the demands were the heaviest, Jesus could be found praying. That says something pretty profound about him.

The Application

If you think about it, there are a lot of things that we need to do in a day. There's school, with assignments, tests, readings and writing; there's getting to school by bus or car or walking; there's after school, with sports, friends, food, homework and parents. We really are very busy, aren't we? Sometimes it feels like there is so much to do and so little time to do it. Sometimes it feels like the tasks are overwhelming. Sometimes it feels like people are making demands of us that we just can't live up to.

Isn't it interesting that Jesus started off his day by praying! He knew that to get done what needed doing, he would need some help. So the question is, do you know who will help you get through it all? It's humbling to realize that there are some things you can't do on your own.

The point is that taking some time at the beginning of your day to talk with God allows you to ask God for wisdom (like for that math test coming up) and it reminds you throughout the day that God is walking with you.

Try this—write out your prayers in the journal pages and as you write them, speak them to God. They will serve as good reminders of "where you've been" in life and how God has walked with you.

Jesus knew that hooking up with God first thing in his day kept him on track for the rest of it. Try it and see what happens!

My thoughts to the Master

A Forgiving Faith

Scripture: Mark 2:1-12

Key Verse: "I, even I, am he who blots out your transgressions, for my own sake, and remembers your sins no more. *(Isaiah 43:25)*

About the Passage

When the Gospels were written, all the writers, Mark included, followed a certain pattern of writing (this is kinda like a mini-English class!). For example, when they told a miracle story, the story followed a particular structure and contained several elements. First, the setting is laid out, then a problem arises. A solution to that problem is provided along with evidence of that solution. Why am I talking about this, you ask? Simple! The miracle story you just read follows that basic pattern but ends up with a strange twist!

Jesus is in a house packed with people (setting). Some guys come through the roof with a friend who can't walk (problem). Jesus sees the faith of this man's friends and solves the problem by forgiving his sins (solution?)! The twist on this is that the men who lowered their friend through the roof to see Jesus had one thing on their minds—that Jesus would make their friend walk! But instead, Jesus forgives the man's sins. Jesus understood that this man's deepest need was not to walk but to be forgiven. The religious leaders argue with Jesus about forgiving sins and Jesus asks, " which is easier, healing a man or forgiving his sins?" The point is that the price Jesus paid to forgive our sins was tremendous—a much more difficult and painful task than healing.

One more point, did you notice that the lame man doesn't actually show any signs of faith? When Jesus forgives based on faith, it's the faith of the man's friends! Now perhaps the lame man had faith, we don't know. But it's significant that Jesus forgave a person's sins based on the faith of that person's friends.

A Walk on the Wild Side: Walking with the Master

The Application

Sometimes during my growing up years, I thought my parents didn't understand what I needed. They didn't seem to know what my life was like. They would often tell me, "We're just doing what's best for you." Now that I'm older, I see that my parents did understand me better than I thought—not that they were always right but they had some pretty good advice.

In the Scripture passage, Jesus was asked to heal a man. But Jesus knew what this man needed more than healing, he needed forgiveness from his sins. I can just imagine the man's reaction to Jesus' words "Your sins are forgiven." "That's great Jesus, but what about my legs here!"

What kind of stuff do you bring to God in your prayers? Do you pray for family members, friends, school, church, etc.? It's great for you to bring stuff before God. It's good to have faith that God will answer your prayers. He wants to hear about it—he really cares about what you're going through. Once you've given those things to God, you have to trust him to do what's best. He knows what is going to be the ideal result for you and so you have to have faith that the decision he makes will be the right one. Even though you may think that God is totally unaware of how things work down here he's doing what's best for you.

Remember, your faith can make a difference in the lives of your family and friends. So if you have a friend who's hurting, take a risk and lower him/her through the roof so Jesus can work in their life too!

My thoughts to the Master

A Place for Everyone

Scripture: Mark 2:13-22

Key Verse: It is not the healthy who need a doctor, but the sick. I have not come to call the righteous but the sinners. *(Mark 2:17)*

About the Passage

Tax collectors weren't the most popular people in Jesus' day. In fact, they were even kicked out of the synagogue. Come to think of it, they aren't the most popular people today either. Not many people appreciate a person who comes to their door and says, "Give me your money." But it's exactly this fact that makes this passage so wild. Jesus goes to Levi (a.k.a. Matthew), the local tax collector, and asks him to become one of his disciples.

The Pharisees must have loved this one. Here Jesus thinks he's this big religious leader and he associates with sinful people. However, Jesus' answer shuts them up pretty quickly. By calling Levi, Jesus does a couple of things. First, he says that the message he has is for everyone, not just a chosen few. You see, the Pharisees believed that in order to get to God you had to follow laws and rules, and anyone who didn't was considered a "sinner." But Jesus shows that the way to God is open to everyone and all it takes is to get up and go when Christ says, "Follow me." The Pharisees never imagined that God would want to associate with those who did not follow all the laws. They couldn't picture a person different from them in God's kingdom.

Secondly, Jesus shows us that sometimes it is most difficult for those who think they are righteous to accept the gospel message. Just as a healthy person will never go to the doctor for medication, a person who believes they have all the answers will never look to God for help. They couldn't understand that all of us need help. We all have sinned and fall short of the glory of God (read Romans 3:22-23).

The Application

This passage has a lot to say about your own relationship with God. For one, you need to know that wherever you are in life, God loves you and wants to get to know you. It also says that just "doing what's right" isn't enough and that there needs to be a personal commitment and desire to get to know Christ. But what we want to focus on is something that goes beyond just your personal relationship.

Our culture today is plagued by racism. Racism has been present throughout time. The Pharisees thought that those who didn't follow the law were inferior and God could not love these same people. Likewise, racism creeps into our churches. Have you ever looked at someone in church and wondered what they were doing there? Maybe they didn't dress right, or their hair was all messed up, or they kinda smelled. Remember, these are the types of people Jesus hung out with—the ones that didn't fit!

Racism doesn't stop in the church. It's in schools, on playgrounds, on sports teams. It's found in little things like laughing at someone's clothes, ignoring someone at lunchtime or mocking someone behind their back. God loves all creation and he wants every one of us to love him in return.

It's dangerous when racism shapes the way you think because you spend so much time looking down on someone that you miss seeing how good they are. The Pharisees didn't see how God's love was meant for everyone and so they missed out on God's love altogether. Face it, we all need God whether we are good-looking or not-so-good-looking. Why not spend your energy loving others instead of hiding God's love from the people you meet?

My thoughts to the Master

The Sabbath: What is it Anyway?

Scripture: Mark 2:23-3:6

Key Verse: "Observe the Sabbath day by keeping it holy, as the LORD your God has commanded you. Six days you shall labor and do all your work, but the seventh day is a Sabbath to the LORD your God." (Deut. 5:12-14)

About the Passage

Have you ever wondered about keeping the Sabbath? You probably know it's one of the Ten Commandments. And you probably have read parts of the Bible where Jesus seemingly disobeys Sabbath laws. So is it really that important? In Jesus' time, Sabbath laws were very strict. Even today, devout Jews follow a very rigid pattern of Sabbath observance. For example, all meals must be prepared ahead of time and only a certain number of steps may be taken. Deuteronomy 5:12-15 (the fourth commandment) spells out very clearly that work must be done in six days and the seventh day is intended for rest.

So what were Jesus and his disciples doing in that grain field anyway? (It seems that the Pharisees are always following Jesus.) Didn't Jesus know what the Sabbath was about? Did he finally slip up? Well, Jesus did have a clear understanding of the Sabbath—much clearer than the Pharisees did. He knew that "the Sabbath was made for humankind, and not humankind for the Sabbath" (Mark 2:27 NRSV).

The Pharisees were not fulfilling the intent of the Sabbath. They felt it was just another tradition that needed to be followed in order to maintain God's favor. The purpose of the Sabbath was to give people a chance to rest and restore their spirit. Jesus knew that, for the Pharisees, following the letter of the law was more important than upholding the purpose of the law. In fact, when Jesus asked whether it was more important to heal a man's hand or follow the law, the Pharisees were more concerned with the law than the man's well being. I doubt that the Pharisees got much rest on the Sabbath!

A Walk on the Wild Side: Walking with the Master

The Application

Do you "celebrate" the Sabbath? You should! It seems like such a foreign term doesn't it—it's such a "Bible" word. But the Sabbath is really an important part of our lives. Granted that the Sabbath is actually Saturday and we choose Sunday as our day of rest but the principle remains the same. God knew it was important for humankind to rest—something that many of us forget to do. We live in a culture that defines success by how many appointments you have on your calendar or by how many "double-bookings" you have in a day. Everything has been tailored to suit our busy lifestyles: fast food, fast cars, pagers, e-mail, faxes, one-hour photo, Sunday shopping. For me, however, the cell phone is the pinnacle of this. No matter where you are, you can be reached. You can be in your car, in a meeting, watching TV, eating supper, traveling to Timbuktu, sitting on the "throne"—it doesn't matter, someone can always bother you. There's something not right about that!

The Sabbath is about resting. The fourth commandment doesn't make it an option—you WILL rest on the Sabbath! There needs to be a time each week when you can relax, re-energize yourself and spend time worshipping God with other believers—it does the body good! In your journal, write down all the things you have to do in the next week, making sure you leave space for the Sabbath. If you can't do all your tasks in seven days, including a time to celebrate the Sabbath, then I would say you're doing too much!

24 **A Walk on the Wild Side:** Walking with the Master

My to do list

A Walk on the Wild Side: Walking with the Master

My thoughts to the Master

The Price of Success

Scripture: Mark 3:7-13

Key Verse: "But what about you?" he asked. "Who do you say I am?" Peter answered, "You are the Christ." *(Mark 8:29)*

About the Passage

I find it interesting how many times Mark writes, "Jesus withdrew" or "Jesus went up a mountain" or "Jesus went off by himself." It seems that everywhere Jesus went, there were people following him. Often they were not just following but crowding, pushing and clamoring just to get a look. No wonder he wanted to be alone every once in a while.

In this passage there are three significant groups of people. Each group understood Jesus differently. One group is "the crowd." The crowd wanted to see Jesus but wanted to see him for all the wrong reasons. The reports that there was a man who could heal diseases and make people walk spread quickly. So every person who had ever hoped for a better life came to Jesus to find it. The crowd longed for this man, longed for a better life. But what Mark lets us know is that they really had no idea who he was.

The second group we won't deal with too much now. They were the spirits. They recognized who Jesus was and were terrified by it. When they cry out, "You are the Son of God," it is not a statement of faith in Christ but one of fear. They knew that the authority Jesus held covered more than just diseases and ailments.

The third group in this passage is the disciples. Look at verse 13 again and notice that Jesus called those whom he wanted to teach to himself. Did they know who he was? Were they more intelligent than the rest? There is nothing to indicate that the Twelve were brilliant scholars. In fact, even the disciples didn't recognize who Jesus really was. But they were committed to following him. They were willing to sacrifice for him. That's the quality Jesus saw in them and that is why he called them aside and wanted to teach them his ways.

A Walk on the Wild Side: Walking with the Master

The Application

One of the most frustrating things about today's culture is "the trend!" One day you go out and buy some clothes so you fit in, and the next day you're totally out of style. Even the seemingly unchangeable blue jeans are subject to "the trend." What would happen if you followed every trend that came up? If bell-bottoms were in—you'd love 'em! If skateboarding was in—you'd love it! If jumping off bridges was in—you'd jump! In all your "trend following," you would end up finding out that you really love nothing at all. Your commitment would only be to "the trend."

That must be how Jesus felt about the crowd. Their commitment was to find a better way of life for themselves and whoever could provide it at the time was their best friend. So even though Jesus was popular, he knew the commitment of the crowd was to themselves, not to him. Sometimes our lives are like that too, aren't they? Even when we worship, there are times when it feels so great. The music's awesome and everyone's praising and jumping up and down and it makes us feel good. But other times, it isn't so hot and sometimes you wish you weren't there. If that happens to you, do a check-up on your heart and see if it's the experience you're committed to or the God you're worshipping. Remember that the reason for worship is to glorify God, not for our personal gratification. When you're commitment is to Christ, no matter what the situation, you will find that he will call you to himself and teach you who he really is.

My thoughts to the Master

Devotional #10

Calling all Disciples

Scripture: Mark 3:14-19

Key Verse: Then Jesus came to them and said, "All authority in heaven and on earth has been given to me. Therefore go and make disciples of all nations, baptizing them in the name of the Father and of the Son and of the Holy Spirit, and teaching them to obey everything I have commanded you. And surely I am with you always, to the very end of the age." *(Matt. 28:18-20)*

About the Passage

Jesus calls to himself those who have made a commitment to him. In teaching the twelve disciples, Jesus recognizes that even though these people are not perfect, they desire to walk as he does. Remember that the Twelve were simple people, living simple lives before Jesus called them. They were fishermen and tax collectors. Yet, because of their desire for God, Christ passed on to them the authority to preach and cast out demons.

The three basic parts to this passage are "call," "equip," and "name." We'll take a look at the last two. Christ knew the disciples would need specific equipment in order to be effective as his apostles. They would need to be effective preachers so that people would listen. They would need to be able to deal with the demons and spirits that were wreaking havoc in people's lives. So Jesus didn't merely send them out, he filled their lives with the gifts and abilities they would need to get the job done.

While he was on earth, people were able to see God through the person of Jesus. This passage shows us that God also makes himself known through us— he sends us out as his messengers and ambassadors so people are able to see God through us. That's pretty wild!

The naming of the disciples is important. It identifies them as individuals with specific gifts and talents. Each person, as an individual, is an important part of the whole. Now, we aren't told what the specific talents and gifts of the individuals are but we do know these people were given a specific role that would help achieve the goal of bringing the message of God to the whole world!

The Application

Do you know what your gifts are? I am always surprised by the fact that many people have no idea. When it comes to determining where your giftedness lies, a good place to start is with the things you enjoy doing. Do you enjoy speaking in public? Are you musical? Do friends and peers come to you just to talk? Are you extremely organized? Do you love working with small children? It is important that you come to some understanding of how God has equipped you to serve.

Here's an exercise for your journal. Create a chart with three columns. In the first, make a list of the things you enjoy doing. Don't include silly things like "I like torturing my brother!" or "I like eating!" In the second column, list the things you feel you are good at. Some people have a real hard time with that because they think they are bragging. But remember, you are listing the ways God has equipped you to be his worker. So you're bragging for God, not yourself. Then, in the third column, think of some ways you can use those gifts to serve God. Maybe that means the way you use them in the church or perhaps in your school. And then, if you dare, show that list to your pastor, parents or youth worker. Ask them to help you put these gifts to use.

Remember, everyone has talents. But those who use those talents to serve God by serving people around them turn those talents into spiritual gifts. Make good use of the way God has equipped you – he's depending on you!

A Walk on the Wild Side: Walking with the Master

My gifts

My thoughts to the Master

He's Crazy, I Tell You!

Scripture: Mark 3:20-35

Key Verse: Then he looked at those seated in a circle around him and said, "Here are my mother and my brothers! Whoever does God's will is my brother and sister and mother." *(Mark 3:34-35)*

About the Passage

It's not hard to see how Jesus' fame and reputation is spreading. There seems to be no place where he can find peace and quiet. Even in a house (or "at home" as some other translations put it), he is mobbed by the crowd. Interestingly enough, his family comes and tries to straighten things out because Jesus obviously has no idea what to do! Again, the question of Jesus' true identity is raised. His family does not know who he is, nor do the Scribes and Pharisees when they start accusing him of being in league with the devil.

Jesus' answer to these accusations is quite clear. "If I am Satan," he says, "why am I throwing out Satan's demons? Can a person who is doing everything possible to lose, win?" It's like saying, "I'm going to win this basketball game but I will only shoot on my own hoop!" The accusation made by the Pharisees just doesn't make sense.

Verse 29 talks about the "unpardonable sin," the one sin that cannot be forgiven. The point Jesus is making here is if you confuse God's work with Satan's work, you will be outside of God's forgiveness. Or another way to say it, if you look around and see creation, miracles, people being saved and believe that it is not God, but Satan who is doing this, forgiveness will not be with you.

The last word in the passage opens up the work and saving grace of Jesus to everyone. He says that those who have a passion to know and do God's will are the ones who are in his family. (Talk to your pastor if you want more information about this topic.)

The Application

I love doing "Random Acts of Senseless Kindness" with youth groups. What I love the most about them is the expressions on people's faces when we do these totally "out-of-the-blue" things. They must think we're from another planet.

That must have been how Jesus felt. Jesus' life revolved around something different than most of ours do. He had different priorities, a different perspective than most. Jesus struggled to do the Father's will. We seem to fight more with our own will than with God's. It is because of this difference that most people will say that Jesus was insane, or literally "beside himself."

Think about this for a minute: who is "beside himself" Jesus or us? I think Jesus has this "living thing" down and we have it turned around. He knows what's really important in life and we seem to be running around like a chicken without a head!

To live as Jesus did, you need to step out and take a walk on the wild side. You need to walk alongside Jesus and take some risks. The way Jesus asks us to live is something that the world doesn't understand. Putting others before yourself, becoming last, not concerning yourself with possessions, that's just "crazy talk" to the world. You need to be "beside yourself" for God! It may not be easy because people might look at you as if you're crazy. Even the people closest to you may not recognize what has happened in your life. But Christ will know, and will say, "Because of your willingness to do my Father's will, you are my brother, my sister."

My thoughts to the Master

What Kind of Ground are You?

Scripture: Mark 4:1-20

Key Verse: So is my word that goes out from my mouth: It will not return to me empty, but will accomplish what I desire and achieve the purpose for which I sent it. *(Isaiah 55:11)*

About the Passage

Most of you will recognize the parable of the sower in today's passage. Parables were stories Jesus used to relay a message or a truth to those who heard it. Basically, it is a story with a deeper meaning. Every person who reads the parables of Jesus has an opportunity to interpret what is really being said. So think for a second about what this parable is saying to you. It's important that before you go on, you think for yourself what the parable is saying. Go on, take two minutes, I'll wait!

The parable of the sower is unique because Jesus actually interprets the story for us. This fact allows us to look even deeper into the passage. It gives us a glimpse of the type of crowd following Jesus.

So here's my interpretation of the parable. The seed is the gospel message. Some people are not very thirsty to hear God's word. They hear it but make no effort to understand it and when Satan comes along with something more exciting they forget all about God. Some really want to learn and grow but have no discipline or endurance to stay with it. As soon as they get tired of it, they let it die. Others hear and accept God's good news but do nothing about changing their lives. So all the old things in their life "choke" out the new life God is offering. Finally, there are those who want to hear the gospel and make every effort to understand it. They take the seed they have been given and nurture it so that it will grow and become strong. Their hard work pays off as the gospel not only grows in their lives but branches out to the lives of the people around them.

A Walk on the Wild Side: Walking with the Master

The Application

I want to simply ask the question "What kind of ground are you?" In your journal, make headings for each type of ground you find in the parable of the sower. Under these headings, write your own interpretation of what you think Jesus is trying to say. Then place yourself under one of these types of ground. What do you need to do to become the ground that opens up, accepts, and nurtures the message that God has given?

Make sure you take time to pray about it!!

What kind of ground are you ?

My thoughts to the Master

Listening to What Counts

Scripture: Mark 4:1-20

Key Verse: The fear of the Lord—that is wisdom, and to shun evil is understanding. *(Job 28:28)*

About the Passage

Sometimes there just is not enough space to say everything that needs to be said about a certain passage. This is the case with Mark 4:1-20. Let's take a look at this passage from another angle. Look at verse 12. Do you notice anything strange about it? Does anything about that verse bother you? What strikes me is the fact that it seems to be saying that God is deliberately hiding the truth from some people. Jesus says he speaks in parables so people will hear but not necessarily understand. That's a tough thing to hear from Jesus' mouth and for many of us, it doesn't fit the picture we have of him.

This passage does say something about the sovereignty of God, doesn't it? It reminds us that "his ways are not our ways, and his thoughts not our thoughts" (Isa. 55:8) and that many times we will not understand the ways of God. That's where faith comes in.

Another way to look at the passage is to say that faith in God is not simply a good feeling. Jesus spoke to the crowd about the Kingdom of God but he knew many of them were not interested; they just wanted their wounds healed. He also knew that those who truly desired to know him would dig deeper and find the meaning behind the story. In essence, Jesus is saying that faith in God is not for those who follow for personal gain. It is for those who have the discipline and desire to look deep into his Word and find understanding. Perhaps, in your searching, you won't find anything. But know that God also honors a desire and commitment to him. Notice how the disciples didn't understand what Jesus was saying but he took them aside, apart from the rest of the crowd, and explained to them saying, "You are permitted to understand the secret about the Kingdom of God" (4: 9 NLT).

A Walk on the Wild Side: Walking with the Master

The Application

Have you ever felt that God is far away from you? Did you ever feel that you were all alone with no one you could turn to? The reality of life is that there are down times. There will be times when you feel ineffective, "un-spiritual," or just plain sinful. It's at times like this that we tend to give up on God because he doesn't seem to care.

If you take the passage you just read seriously, it's saying that when you feel farthest away from God and nothing seems to make sense, that's when you need to look the hardest. Think of homework for a second (sorry)—when you don't get a math problem or can't understand what the teacher is saying, do you just say forget it and walk away? No, you go to the teacher and ask questions. You use all your brainpower to solve the problem. It's the same way with Christianity. When things don't seem to make sense, you need to look hard for the answer. Remember, Jesus said there will be many who hear the message but only a few will understand and act on it. Don't just hear the words, understand them!

Here's what I want you to do. In your journal, write down questions about God, Jesus, Christianity, the Bible, church, etc. Then discuss them with your pastor or your parents or some else you trust. Having questions or things you don't understand isn't bad. Not putting the effort into finding solutions is!

My questions about God, Jesus, Christianity, the Bible, church, etc.

My thoughts to the Master

Devotional #14: Never Gonna Be As Big As Jesus

Scripture: Mark 4:21-34; 6:6b-13

Key Verse: Again he said, "What shall we say the kingdom of God is like, or what parable shall we use to describe it? It is like a mustard seed, which is the smallest seed you plant in the ground. Yet when planted, it grows and becomes the largest of all garden plants, with such big branches that the birds of the air can perch in its shade." *(Mark 4:30-32)*

About the Passage

These three parables talk about one of the most amazing, and yet, confusing aspects of the Christian faith. The first is the lamp on the stand. This is pretty straight forward, isn't it? For a flame to survive it needs to be exposed to air. If you put it under something, the light eventually dies. If you hold it out, it grows and becomes stronger. So Jesus is saying, if the light you have (God's light and love), is kept private and secret so no one sees it, it will die out. But if you let this light shine so everyone can see it, it will grow and become brighter and brighter.

In the same breath, Jesus tells two more parables about the Kingdom of God. The one seems to say that the Kingdom of God is much bigger than just you and me. We have a part to play in it, but God's Kingdom is not dependent on us. Like a seed, we may drop it in the ground, but we have very little to do with its growing and becoming a fully developed plant. The gospel message (the seed), has a power all of its own; a power that does not rely on humans for its success (remember Isaiah 55:11 from devotion #12).

The last of the parables is along the same lines as the second one but with some subtle differences. The Kingdom of God may have small beginnings but it will eventually grow into something huge. It's easy to get discouraged by the seemingly minimal size of God's Kingdom in relation to the whole world. But, like the mustard seed, the Kingdom will grow and grow and become a mighty and effective force in the world. What the world perceives as weakness, is the Kingdom's greatest strength.

A Walk on the Wild Side: Walking with the Master

The Application

I used to feel guilty over the fact that I wasn't bringing people to Christ. I was a Christian and I attended church and I even had some non-Christian friends but I felt I wasn't doing any of that Great Commission stuff! But the most frustrating part was that when I did talk to other people about God, they didn't immediately turn and give their lives over to him. I had all this guilt but it didn't seem to be doing any good!

I have a feeling that many of you may feel the same way at times. We know that God calls us to tell others about him and we hear stories of people walking out on the street and bringing 18 people to God in 4 minutes! Why doesn't it happen like that for us? Remember back to the passage that you just read. It basically says these things:
- Do all you can to show others you're a Christian.
- Remember that God is the one who will turn people to himself, not you.
- All you need to do is plant the seed and it will grow on its own. You may feel the seed you have is small and weak but give it time and it will explode into a powerful force.

Remember that it's all about guilt and patience; or I should say, NOT having guilt and practicing lots of patience. You make sure your light is shining bright and let God do the rest.

My thoughts to the Master

Faith When Things Seem Stormy

Scripture: Mark 4:35-41

Key Verse: Who has gone up to heaven and come down? Who has gathered up the wind in the hollow of his hands? Who has wrapped up the waters in his cloak? Who has established all the ends of the earth? What is his name, and the name of his son? Tell me if you know! (Proverbs 30:4)

About the Passage

Jesus' disciples (many were fishermen) knew the dangers the Sea of Galilee held. They were familiar with the sudden storms that crashed upon the lake and they were afraid! At the same time, they must have been frustrated with Jesus. They were just beginning to understand and see who he really was and then he did this. In the midst of danger, the Master was sleeping.

I have to wonder what Jesus' facial expression was when he was asked, "Don't you care?" It is a question that demands an answer. He immediately answered it by calming the wind and the waves. He eventually answered it by hanging on a cross.

Again, the question of Jesus' identity is brought to the forefront. In the past, Jesus displayed his authority over evil spirits and even sin. In this passage we are reminded that, as the creator, he had authority over the wind, waves and rain. The disciples' question showed that they had no idea who he was. The answer became clear as they continued to question "Who is this?"

It is tough to give a clear definition to the word "faith." Words like trust, depend, believe, hope, all come to mind immediately. But here's a question I want to leave you with. Would you be able to define faith as "just knowing he's there?" Look at the passage again. Perhaps true faith means that knowing Jesus is with you in the storm, no matter what he's doing, is enough to put your mind at ease.

The Application

I would assume that most of you are familiar with the poem "Footprints." It is the story of a woman who sees her life flash before her. Along the way, there are two sets of footprints, one her own and one belonging to God. At the most difficult times in her life, however, she notices there is only one set of prints. Upset, she asks the Lord why this is. The reply comes, "My precious, precious child, that is when I carried you."

The passage we read today teaches us that faith is more than just believing in God. It's trusting that, even when it seems he's not there, he will take care of you. There are times in our lives when God feels far away, when it seems he has hit the snooze button too many times. That is when your faith comes under its greatest test. That is when you have to ask yourself "Do I really know who Jesus is and, if I do, do I trust him?"

Deuteronomy 31:6 says that God will never leave nor forsake us; it's a promise! The disciples weren't satisfied with Jesus' presence alone, they needed him to be doing something, to make things better. But when life is at its stormiest, remember two things. One is that God loves you very much and wants only the best for you. The second is that he has promised to always be with you, no matter how far away he seems to be. Put those two together and I'd say you have a pretty good formula for faith in God.

My thoughts to the Master

Devotional #16

Christianity & Beyond!

Scripture: Mark 5:1-20

Key Verse: For I am convinced that neither death nor life, neither angels nor demons, neither the present nor the future, nor any powers, neither height nor depth, nor anything else in all creation, will be able to separate us from the love of God that is in Christ Jesus our Lord. (Romans 8:38-39)

About the Passage

A key element of this passage is introduced to us in the first verse. It says that Jesus got in a boat and crossed to the other side of the lake. "Wow, that's really interesting!" you say. Just bear with me. There are clues in the rest of the passage which will explain why this is so significant. Here are the clues: pigs, evil spirit, tombs (un-kosher items). The question is "Where is Jesus?" The answer is that he is outside of Jewish territory, in Gentile country. You need to understand that in those days, each country or even town was believed to have its own god. When one country invaded and defeated another, the god of the losing country was vanquished.

As Yahweh's chosen people, the Israelites believed he was "their" god. But in this passage we see Jesus going into "foreign" territory and bringing order and healing to a place of chaos and death. Jesus shows that God is sovereign, not only in Israel, but around the world. He also shows that not only has God come to bless and heal the Jewish people, but all peoples. The first readers of this passage would have known this was a pretty wild act on Jesus' part. It described that they can never control God and never know exactly what he is going to do or where he is going to do it. Jesus also showed them that no matter what or where God acts, it will be for the healing and well being of the people. The authority and power of God knows no bounds! It was an important lesson then and is equally important now.

A Walk on the Wild Side: Walking with the Master

The Application

Have you ever played "Capture the Flag?" Here's how it works. A large area is divided into two territories and as long as you are on "your side," you are safe, no one can capture you. However, when you make the trek over into enemy territory, you are "fair game!" Anyone who is on the other team, can capture you and throw you into jail. You have lots of power on your side of the field, but none on the other. That's how a Jew would have felt in Gentile territory and visa versa. In fact, Jews even looked down on people from Samaria, which is in northern Israel, because they were half Jew, half Gentile. When Jews traveled from north to south, they chose to take the much longer route around Samaria rather than saving time by going through it. We don't quite have that same understanding of boundaries here in Canada.

What you need to remember is that the power of God is not restricted to one particular location. We can't say that God is only here in church, or only in Canada or the US. The message of grace and redemption is meant for all people, from evangelicals in Winnipeg to tribal peoples in Africa. There is no place where God is "out of place."

That has far reaching implications for our lives. It means that there is no one who is unworthy of hearing the Gospel. The "universality" of Christ's power also gives us the confidence to bring the message into those places where it may not be so welcome. In your journal, write down specific places where you fear talking about God. Pray that God would bring the message there. Then be ready to go!

My thoughts to the Master

For the Love of Pigs!

Scripture: Mark 5:1-20

Key Verse: "So do not worry, saying, 'What shall we eat?' or 'What shall we drink?' or 'What shall we wear?' For the pagans run after all these things, and your heavenly Father knows that you need them." (Matthew 6:31-32)

About the Passage

There is something in Mark 5:1-20 that deserves a second look. The far-reaching power of Jesus is important but the pigs teach a valuable lesson too. There are two remarkable things which happen here. One is that a man, who is basically killing himself, is healed when a legion of demons is cast out of him. The second is that the spirits are allowed to possess the herd of pigs that is nearby and 2,000 pigs rush into the lake and drown. No fiction writer could think of something this wild!

But what is equally wild is the reaction of the crowd. People came rushing to see what happened (I assume 2,000 pigs jumping into a lake would cause quite a commotion) and they observed the "wild" man sitting there in his right mind. The onlookers saw the man, and were afraid! They were told about the pigs and got upset, begging Jesus to leave the area. One would have expected celebration and thankfulness but instead, there was fear and a discomfort with the presence of Jesus.

The question of why Jesus allowed demons to possess and destroy all that pork is a question we won't answer today. But isn't it interesting that the reaction of the people seems to say they are more concerned with the drowning of the pigs than with the healing of a man. It seems to me they were quite comfortable with the way things were and Jesus coming in and dealing with evil spirits just screwed things up. Sure it may have worked out for that possessed guy but what about all the money the other people lost? It seems these people switched the great commandment around to read, "Love your PIG as yourself!"

The Application

What or who are the pigs in your life? "Well," you say, "there's my brother and..." No, that's not what I mean! What are the things in your life that you value more highly than your relationship with God? If you're not sure, a good test is to think of one item in your life that you value. Line that item up with your relationship with God. If you had to give one up, which would it be? For you it may be friends, money, clothes, slurpees and the list goes on.

Take a look at Matthew 6:24. "No one can serve two masters. Either he will hate the one and love the other, or he will be devoted to the one and despise the other. You cannot serve both God and Money." The word money is actually "mammon" which can mean money, wealth, belongings, etc. The fact is, there is only one thing that can be "Lord" of your life. You need to make a decision what that is going to be.

You may have heard of Saint Francis of Assisi. He was born into a rich family and had it all. Gradually, however, he become disillusioned with his wealth and renounced all his inheritance. He stripped off his clothes and walked into the countryside to live as a hermit, repairing churches and ministering to the poor (he did put on some clothes again, though).

I'm not suggesting that you need to do this but Francis knew that in order to serve God, he needed to get rid of all worldly distractions. He knew God came before "pigs." What are the things you value more highly than your relationship with God? Take some time to talk to God about them and ask him for help with setting priorities.

My thoughts to the Master

The Touch of Faith

Scripture: Mark 5:21-43

Key Verse: He said to her, "Daughter, your faith has healed you. Go in peace and be freed from your suffering." *(Mark 5:34)*

About the Passage

This passage has several important things to say about faith and healing.
- The plea of Jarius for the healing of his daughter is significant. Here is another case of one person's faith healing or saving another. Notice that Jarius seems to be absolutely convinced that Jesus can heal his daughter.
- The Key Verse, "Daughter, your faith has healed you," is also significant. The woman was convinced that if she could just get a touch of Jesus' robe, she would be made well and the results were immediate.
- The crowd felt all hope was lost because the girl was already dead. But Jesus said, "Don't be afraid, just believe." When Jesus claimed the girl was only sleeping, the crowd's faith (or lack thereof) came to light as they laughed at him.

Amidst all the displays of faith, something needs to be said about the verses that are missing from this passage. These are the verses that say, "when everyone saw how the woman was healed, they too had faith and touched Jesus;" or "the fact that a woman was healed through touching Jesus gave everyone confidence in the healing of the girl despite her death." Rather, we read verse 31 which has the disciples saying, "With so many people clamoring around and touching you, how can you ask 'Who touched me'?" Why is it that the crowd has enveloped Jesus in anticipation of miraculous signs, yet nothing happens when they bump and rub shoulders with him. But a woman can crawl meekly through the crowd, just touch the hem of his cloak and be healed? Remember that part of faith is recognizing who Jesus is. Jesus' power is far greater than even the limits of human life. Jesus proved his authority was greater than the confines of mortality and was greater than the expectations of "the crowd." God honors those who come to him in "desperate" faith; those who say "all-or-nothing!"

A Walk on the Wild Side: Walking with the Master

The Application

Are you beginning to see a pattern in the Gospel of Mark? There are themes that reappear over and over again. I read this passage a few years ago and was struck in a new way. I felt like I was one of the people in the crowd. I was around Jesus, I knew him, I would bump into him once and a while and we might even talk. I would see people who would crawl up to him just to touch him and they would walk away changed. Why was I so close and yet unchanged by his presence?

The change occurs in the risking with God. My prayer life changed and I began asking God for specific things, for healing, for salvation for friends, for help to get through tight months. I asked because I knew God could do it! Did God always answer my prayers the way I wanted? No, but I found I gained confidence not only in talking with God but in talking to friends and others about God.

Do you think that the woman who touched Jesus' cloak or Jarius' daughter never had problems after that? Of course they did, but they also had someone they could turn to when things got tough; someone who had the power to deal with every situation. Take a risk in your life. Let go of everything you feel you "need" to hold on to and give God everything. Just like the woman who touched Jesus, your cry of faith will not go unnoticed!

58 **A Walk on the Wild Side:** Walking with the Master

My thoughts to the Master

A Walk on the Wild Side: Walking with the Master

Home Court Dis-advantage!

Devotional #19

Scripture: Mark 6:1-6

Key Verse: Jesus said to them, "Only in his hometown, among his relatives and in his own house is a prophet without honor." *(Mark 6:4)*

About the Passage

I have to admit that I spent some time pondering whether or not I should deal with this particular passage. Eventually, I came to the conclusion that I should (obviously). BECAUSE? The passage is a familiar one and I pray that its familiarity won't distract from a good learning opportunity.

As Jesus taught in his hometown synagogue, he amazed everyone with his teaching. The questions the people were asking were almost ridiculous. They wondered, "Why can Jesus do all this stuff and I can't?" These were the people who grew up with Jesus, who played together with him and went to the same schools. They knew Jesus didn't go off to seminary and receive degrees in theology. They knew he was a carpenter, an ordinary man making a simple living much like themselves. So how did he know all this stuff?

The whole problem with the situation was that they were so busy wondering about Jesus that they didn't listen to a word he was saying. The fact that Jesus could talk like this offended them. Interestingly enough, their offensive attitude towards Jesus prevented some miracles from taking place (other than a few healings). Did the disbelief of these people make God's power useless? Was Jesus powerless because of the people's lack of faith? No, but it is interesting to realize the "dampening" effect of unbelief on Christ's work. Jesus knew that to stay and try to convince these people would be hopeless. So rather than stay and argue, he moved on. The "stubborn blindness" of Jesus' hometown not only stopped miracles from happening but also prevented them from recognizing his redemptive message.

The Application

One of the biggest problems in many Christian communities today is the plague of complacency. We are very comfortable in the church and don't really want to be disturbed. We are happy with the way things are going and often feel that things don't need to change. One of the messages we get out of today's passage speaks to this issue directly. God can become very familiar to us. We think we know him, we think we know how he thinks, how he works. We talk to him when we need help, like when we didn't study for a test. But for the most part we handle things on our own.

But sometimes strange things happen in church or at youth group and some people get really on fire for God. They want to pray and read the Bible and talk about him to unbelievers. They also look to change the way we do things. Maybe they want different songs or want more Bible studies or longer times for prayer and sharing. Or maybe they want to go out on the streets and invite people to church/youth group and they say we're too stagnant (standing still) and we should do something with our Christianity! Well, when did they get so high and mighty? I can't believe they are accusing us of not doing stuff with our faith! Who do they think they are? Well, I'm not changing; my way of doing it is just fine! I sure hope they leave us alone and let us get on with life!

Oh, don't worry—they'll leave!

A Walk on the Wild Side: Walking with the Master

My thoughts to the Master

Food for the Weary!

Scripture: Mark 6: 7-12,30-44

Key Verse: Now he who supplies seed to the sower and bread for food will also supply and increase your store of seed and will enlarge the harvest of your righteousness. *(2 Corinthians 9:10)*

About the Passage

The combination of these two, somewhat disjointed passages brings the feeding of the 5000 into a new perspective. Don't let the familiarity of the stories stop you from seeing something new in them. Jesus empowers the Twelve to go out and perform all sorts of miraculous works in his name. They are given authority over evil spirits and all kinds of illnesses. Notice how the call for repentance comes before the healings and casting out (verses 12, 13).

From that we jump to the feeding of the 5000. What's important to remember is that the disciples have just come back from teaching and healing and are excited about what happened. They are also tired and hungry and Jesus is very aware of that. However, the cry from the crowds continues and is even stronger. They try to go to a quiet place but are followed by the tenacious crowd. Jesus gives in and begins to teach.

When mealtime came around, the tired, hungry disciples must have been slightly hurt by Jesus' comment that they should get food for the enormous crowd. They may have said something like this, "But Jesus, we've just been healing and saving, and casting out bad guys! Even if we had the energy, we certainly don't have the money!"

The miracle that follows not only provides for the physical needs of the crowd but empowers the disciples as they continue to minister. You see, Jesus knew the limitations of his workers and he also knew that the demands of the task were too great for them. By asking them to feed the 5000, Jesus provides his disciples with the resources and energy to do so.

A Walk on the Wild Side: Walking with the Master

The Application

As you walk the Christian path, you will find there is a tension between BE-ING and DOING. "Being" is the "inside" part of life with God. It is things like praying, worshipping, learning and developing a relationship with him. "Doing" is the active, "outside" part of it. It is helping people in need, telling others about God, showing the Fruit of the Spirit in your life. For one to be effective, the other needs to be healthy. For example, if you have devotions, pray to God and accept his love but do nothing to let others know about it, what good is it? Likewise, if you just do good things all the time, help others, etc. but don't have a relationship with God, what good are all your deeds?

Confused? Overwhelmed? You should be! But, you can find encouragement in today's passage. Even though the disciples were tired from doing good stuff, Jesus asks them to do even more. He asks them to do the impossible! The wild thing is that Jesus fully expects them to do it. It is the same with us. When we get to know Jesus better, he will ask us to do more and more. He may even ask us to do the impossible. But no matter how small you think you are in the big picture, God will provide what you need. He will take care of you. You see, the feeding of the 5000 isn't just about people getting supper, it's about God providing for those who have said, "Yes, I will serve you!" So you may be scared to say "Here I am, send me Lord" but you need to know that he will give you the equipment you need to get the job done, even when you think you don't have anything left!

My thoughts to the Master

It's a Supernatural Relationship

Scripture: Mark 6:45-56

Key Verse: However, as it is written: "No eye has seen, no ear has heard, no mind has conceived what God has prepared for those who love him." *(1 Corinthians 2:9)*

About the Passage

I have found that, of all the stories in the Bible, this is one of the most attractive and familiar to those who are not believers. I think the reason for that is the wild, supernatural nature of the event. Jesus was walking on water as you and I would walk on concrete! Some interpret this passage to mean that, just like Jesus, we can do incredible things like walk on water. Others say it is meant to teach us how Jesus is Lord of heaven and earth. Both of these have some merit.

I think there is another way of looking at it. Jesus is spending time alone with God and the disciples are off to the other side of the lake. (Did the disciples ever wonder how Jesus was going to get to them?) While he is talking with the Father, he sees that the disciples are in trouble. Although the disciples have no idea that Jesus knows their situation, he goes out to meet them. You may be confused by the line "he was about to pass them by..." The NRSV says, "he intended to pass them by." That sounds a bit aloof, doesn't it? The phrase actually stems back to the Old Testament when God would "pass by" the Israelites, letting them know of his presence. It is a revelation of the presence of God.

In this situation, Jesus "passing them by" is a way of letting the disciples know he is there for them. However, when they see him, his appearing doesn't relieve them. Rather, they are terrified by it! Once again, the disciples do not recognize who Jesus is. Instead of being encouraged by Jesus' concern for them, they panic even more. Granted, as a human you don't really expect to see a person walking out on the lake. But then again, if we recognize who Jesus is, nothing should surprise us, should it?

The Application

There are many times when we feel that God isn't concerned about what is going on in our lives. Too often it seems that all he wants us to do is follow him and obey all the rules and guidelines he lays out. If things go wrong in the meantime, well, that's our problem. But the truth is that God is very concerned about our well being. The passage you just read says that even when Jesus was spending time alone, he saw the troubles of his disciples and came to help them. The problem was that, even though the disciples were calling for help, they didn't recognize it when it came.

I remember taking someone out for lunch and hearing that God just was not interested in their life. "He's so far away and I keep asking him to show himself but he doesn't!" So I said, "Well, maybe God is trying to reach you through me!" "No," came the response. "This is your job. You have to do this!"

It is important to understand that God is always interested in what's going on in your life. And if you ask, God will make himself known to you (sometimes even when you don't ask). You just have to be flexible enough to recognize God when he "passes you by!" Anything is possible with him so don't be surprised if, in the midst of a storm, God comes to you and says, "Take courage! It is I!"

My thoughts to the Master

Tradition Rules?

Scripture: Mark 7:1-23

Key Verse: Therefore, there is now no condemnation for those who are in Christ Jesus, because through Christ Jesus the law of the Spirit of life set me free from the law of sin and death. *(Romans 8:1-2)*

About the Passage

Have you ever asked a question and then wished you never asked it because it backfired and blew up in your face? Well, I have a feeling that is how the Pharisees felt when they questioned Jesus about the practices of his disciples. Jewish society was laden with laws that defined how people were to live. The first and most famous of these laws were the Ten Commandments. If you have ever tried to read through the Bible, you will know why most people get bogged down in Leviticus and Numbers. It seems to be law after law after law coming down from God to the people.

As a people who tend to focus more on the New Testament we, at times, view the Old Testament laws as outdated and restrictive. However, these laws had a definite purpose. They were meant to make people aware and keep people away from sin (there's more to it than that, but that's a simple definition). The laws were actually quite freeing because people knew that if they obeyed all these laws it meant they were not sinning! Make sense? Why then, did Jesus seem to disregard all the laws?

Here is where this passage comes in. Jesus challenged the Pharisees (who were terrific law followers) because he knew their hearts were not worshipping God but were worshipping the law. They put more emphasis on faithfulness to the law than to God. In fact, they even used the law to get out of some responsibilities (verses 11-13). So it was not so much the actual law Jesus was reacting to as it was people's abuse of it.

A Walk on the Wild Side: Walking with the Master

The Application

Laws that have been followed faithfully for generations soon become traditions. Everybody has traditions. Families, churches, couples, schools, etc. all have things they do because it has always been done that way. In my family one of my favorite traditions is going to a candlelight service on Christmas Eve and then going to my parents afterwards for a big party, early into the morning! Christmas just wouldn't be the same without it.

Traditions are good because they remind us of special emotions, people, or blessings from the past. But traditions can be dangerous too. Sometimes a tradition can become more important than the actual event you are remembering. Much of the controversy in churches has to do with traditions. Some people would like to see things change while others feel that to change the tradition is to dishonor God. In the church, it is important to remember that in whatever you are doing, God must be glorified in the end. Tradition isn't necessarily bad, but if it becomes more important than God, it's probably time for a change.

A word of caution: we tend to link elderly people with tradition and younger people with change. This is not always true. Young people often hold tightly to something that "has always been that way." Style, music, and appearance can all become gods in themselves quicker than you know. Take some time to write down "traditions" that you hold on to tighter than you do to God. Pray about those things with him!

My thoughts to the Master

On the Road Again!

Scripture: Mark 8:1-21

Key Verse: "Go and proclaim in the hearing of Jerusalem:
"'I remember the devotion of your youth, how as a bride you loved me
and followed me through the desert, through a land not sown.'"
(Jeremiah 2:2)

About the Passage

If there is one thing that encourages me about the Gospel of Mark, it is that the disciples spent all this time with Jesus and still did not clue in to who he really was. I realize that even though I don't always recognize or understand God's ways, he is still willing to work with me! Here we have another miraculous feeding of a large crowd. People followed and listened to Jesus for three days and Jesus was worried that some of them wouldn't make it home because they were so hungry. So he suggested that the disciples feed them. Now, instead of saying, "Great we can see that miracle again," the disciples ask, "Where are we going to get food from? All we have is seven loaves of bread."

The passage is really summed up by the last sentence in verse 21, "Do you still not understand?" The disciples had been walking with Jesus for some time but they failed to truly understand who he was. But what is important to recognize is that Jesus still took time to explain and show signs and wonders to them. Contrast that with the Pharisees who came to Jesus asking for a sign as a test. Jesus did not respond with a sign. He knew their hearts were not focused on finding out more about God but on protecting themselves.

The disciples, though they appear to be kind of stupid, continued to walk with Jesus. They constantly strove to find out who he was. Mark is showing us that the Christian "walk" is a journey—that's why we call it a walk. You are not going to see everything clearly all at once. Evidences and glimpses of who God is may come only a bit at a time. But just as important as finding out who God is, is faithfulness on the journey!

The Application

If you are reading this right now, I want to commend you for it. For what you ask? For the fact that you can read? No. I want to commend you for sticking with your devotions. The Christian journey is like a holiday you take. When you start, you are all excited about traveling and arriving at your destination. When you are close to the end, the excitement grows even more and you seem to have unending energy for the arrival. However, the inbetween part can be a drag sometimes. The excitement of leaving is gone and the anticipation of arriving is still far away.

There's nothing to see, nothing to do, long hours to drive, and everyone in the car is bugging you with every little thing they do. At times, you just want to give up and forget the whole thing. That's a lot like the Christian walk. It's a journey that when you begin, is very exciting and new. Everything is different and there are so many new things to learn. But once you're out of that beginning stage, you find that the "newness" of your experience is gone and the anticipation of what the journey holds dies down a little. You realize that to grow any further is going to take long hours and hard work. . . it's going to take some discipline! Sometimes it seems easier to just give up than to go any further. But you know what God asks of you when it comes to the journey? Stick with it! Keep praying, keep reading the Bible, keep worshipping. You may not understand everything and you may feel you're in over your head, but that's okay. If you're willing to stick with it, God is willing to work with you! You may not see everything clearly now, but once you arrive at your destination, everything will be made clear—gloriously clear!

A Walk on the Wild Side: Walking with the Master

My thoughts to the Master

I Can See

Scripture: Mark 8:22-26

Key Verse: The Spirit of the Sovereign LORD is on me, because the LORD has anointed me to preach good news to the poor. He has sent me to bind up the brokenhearted, to proclaim freedom for the captives and release from darkness for the prisoners, to proclaim the year of the LORD's favor. *(Isaiah 61:1-2)*

About the Passage

"What is happening here? Is Jesus' power failing? Is he not as strong as he once was? Was it too dry in the desert and he didn't have enough spit to heal the man?" These are all questions you may be asking yourself. The placement of this story in the Gospel of Mark is interesting because it comes between the disciples not being able to understand and the great confession of Peter (which you will read about tomorrow). The paradox presented here is that those who can see (the disciples) are blind to who Jesus is. Yet the one who is blind (the blind man—obviously!) is made to see (look at verses 17 & 18 again). But why did Jesus have to touch him twice? Did it not work the first time?

The Christian life is a journey and we will not see everything perfectly the first time we come in contact with Jesus. It is important to be honest about what you can and cannot see. The blind man wasn't satisfied to see "tree-like" people walking around, he wanted to see perfectly. Second best wasn't good enough when it came to his healing. Jesus respected this man's desire and touched him a second time in order to make the healing complete.

By the way, spit was a common healing remedy in Jesus' time. People would rub spit on the afflicted area as a healing balm. However, if you meet someone with a sore on their face, I would not recommend spitting on it!

The Application

If you're looking for strategies on how to get out of answering questions during class, here's one to consider. Have a calm confident look on your face, one that portrays an understanding of the material that is being presented. If you look like you know the answer, be assured you will not be asked any questions. The problem, of course, comes in when you have to write the test. Then you can look anyway you want, it's not going to help!

Since the Christian walk is a journey, you are never going to have all the answers until the very end. In the course of your journey, you will definitely find answers to some of the questions that plague you. But as you grow in Christ you will also gain new questions. And that's okay.

It's important that you are honest about what you see. Glenn Kaiser (Res Band) told a story about a time when he was witnessing to someone. The person asked him a question to which he said, "You know, I don't know the answer to that. Give me some time and I'll find it out though." The person said that Glenn was the first Christian he knew to admit he didn't have all the answers!

Not knowing everything is also the reason we get together as Christians in church, youth group, prayer groups, etc. Together we can look into God's Word and find answers to those questions. So don't worry about not knowing everything about God; just make sure you keep working at finding answers. It's in the midst of that journey that Jesus will touch you again and things will be made clear!

My thoughts to the Master

Devotional #25

Dealing with the Truth

Scripture: Mark 8:27-38

Key Verse: For whoever wants to save his life will lose it, but whoever loses his life for me and for the gospel will save it. *(Mark 8:35)*

About the Passage

We are halfway through Mark! It's interesting to think about what is at the center. We have been talking a lot about who Jesus is and the fact that many people, the disciples included, do not really know. The "Messianic Secret" has been well hidden (see devo #4). However, at the center of the Gospel is Peter's declaration, "You are the Christ, the Anointed One." Finally, the disciples saw who Jesus was, right? Well, kinda, but not really.

For Peter to confess that Jesus was the Messiah was a huge thing. It was understood that the Messiah would be the one who would come and deliver the Jewish people from oppressive rule. They thought the Messiah would be a mighty king, riding in on his steed and wiping out the Romans. The Messiah was no small deal to the Jews. But just like the blind man in yesterday's passage, Peter and the disciples only saw part of the reality.

The fact of the matter is that Jesus was the Messiah and did come to free people from oppressive rule. However, it was the rule of sin and death that he came to conquer; his victory would come through dying. When Jesus explained this to Peter and the others, Peter tried to tell Jesus that he was out of his mind! The disciples, who thought they knew who Jesus was, were forced to reconsider what it meant to follow him. The path that Jesus took was the same one that he asked his disciples to take. That really is the tough thing about discipleship, isn't it? Just as Jesus gave his all for us, he expects us to do the same for the kingdom. The problem for the disciples was that they saw Jesus as someone who would end all their troubles and worries, but when he told them who he really was, they weren't ready to accept that truth!

The Application

If you stop and think about it, it is really quite a scary thing to live the way Jesus asks us to. He is basically saying that there can be nothing more important in your life than living for God! He is saying that even your own life can't be as important as living for God. Throughout the centuries there have been many people who have taken this very seriously. Martyrs are people who have been killed simply because they put God first, above anything. Above family, above possessions, above pain, above their own life. They knew that not only did Jesus die for us, but he asks us the questions, "Would you be willing to die for me?"

We have talked a lot about who Jesus is. But what about who you are? Jesus' life was pretty wild and he calls his followers to live the same way! You see, if you look at Jesus' life and if you want to follow him, you can't just read these stories and say, "Aw, that's so nice!" The Gospel lets us look inside the heart of God so we can pattern our hearts after his.

The bottom line is this: don't say you know who Jesus is if you're not ready to live that out in your life. Don't say, "I want to follow Jesus" and then be surprised when you are asked to give up something for his sake! Being a follower of Christ means that as soon as you recognize and confess who he is, you are recognizing and confessing who YOU are to be.

A Walk on the Wild Side: Walking with the Master

My thoughts to the Master

Devotional #26: A Word from Above

Scripture: Mark 9:2-13

Key Verse: Then a cloud appeared and enveloped them, and a voice came from the cloud: "This is my Son, whom I love. Listen to him!" (Mark 9:7)

About the Passage

If you have attended Sunday school regularly, you will no doubt have a mental image of the transfiguration of Jesus. You know the picture, Jesus with Moses and Elijah on either side of him and they're kinda floating in the air with this bright halo of light around them (I wonder where Star Wars got their "Jedi Fathers" image from?). Well, regardless of what it actually looked like, this was a pretty wild event. Not only was it wild because of what happened but also because of what it meant for the disciples. Remember that the passage before this was Peter's confession that Jesus was the Christ. Not only do three chosen disciples get to see Jesus involved in a supernatural event but they also heard the voice of God declare, "This is my Son, whom I love. Listen to him!" If there has ever been a confirmation from above, that was it!

The other thing that is confirmed by this passage is the 2-in-1 nature of Jesus. It's hard to understand what is meant by Jesus being both human and divine, but here the disciples saw Jesus as both "transcendent" God and suffering human. They saw him talking with Elijah and Moses and heard God's voice. Then in a blink of an eye, they were alone, listening to Jesus talk about his suffering and death.

You may notice that after Peter's confession, everything seemed to point to the Easter story—the death and resurrection of Jesus. This was very deliberate on Mark's part. Notice that even the locations of these stories were all moving closer to Jerusalem. It was all part of Christ's journey, which explains why there was no time to set up shelters. There was work to be done!

The Application

Back when there were only three digits in the year, Christians spent much of their time developing creeds (lists of things they believe). One of the bigger issues dealt with was regarding the humanity and divinity of Christ, the fact that he was both a man and God. One guy, named Apollinarious, said Jesus may have been flesh and blood but his soul was not a human one. This got a lot of Christians upset (rightfully so). So they did what all good Christians should do, formed a committee! They sat down and wrote out what they believed.

The dual nature of Jesus is a big thing. Jesus HAD TO BE both God and human at the same time in order for the plan to work. If he were just human, then he would have died as merely a nice guy. If he was only divine, then he wouldn't have suffered as we do and his "death" would mean nothing. What's the point, you're asking? Here it is: you're learning about a God who not only cares very deeply about you but also understands and feels everything you're going through. Remember, Christ was a teenager, he felt all the same urges and frustrations and confusion you might feel! So don't hesitate to bring it all to him. There's nothing he can't relate to. And as God, he can take all the junk in your life and dump it. If you've never talked to God about taking away junk in your life, do it now. Take a minute to write down in your journal all the things in your life that burden you. Talk to God about those in prayer.

My thoughts to the Master

Powerful Faith

Scripture: Mark 9:4-29

Key Verse: " `If you can'?" said Jesus. "Everything is possible for him who believes." *(Mark 9:23)*

About the Passage

This passage reminds me of being a child. Remember how your mom or dad would show you how to do something and then ask you to try it? Remember trying and trying and not getting it right? Finally your parent has to come and do it for you, again.

When the disciples try to heal a demon-possessed boy, they can't do it. That must have been very frustrating for them since it was only a short time after they were empowered to minister and heal people. But this boy proves to be a problem. Jesus also appears to be frustrated and lectures the disciples about their faith, or lack thereof. The key to the passage lies in the fact that he calls the disciples to bring the boy to him.

You see, the disciples have faith in Jesus. How could they not? Just like Jesus, they had been healing and casting out demons. But as human nature would have it, the disciples forgot who was the source of their power. It was only when the boy is "brought to Christ" that he can be healed.

This passage demonstrates that faith is not power within itself. It is not a magic spell we can cast whenever we feel like it. Our faith always needs to turn our face toward God. When Jesus says, "This kind can only come out by prayer," he is saying that it is only when things are brought before God that they can be dealt with and resolved. Offering prayers to God means you are accepting whatever decision he makes about the situation. I often wonder what the father's response would have been if Jesus chose not to heal the boy. Mark is trying to show us that faith is not a response to what God can do, but a response to who God is!

The Application

The relationship between faith and healing is an interesting one. The Bible tells us and experience shows us that God can heal people. But why is it that today there doesn't seem to be any of that going on? Some people say God has chosen to remain silent until he returns. Others will say it is due to this generation's lack of faith. It's a tricky subject to deal with. There is one thing I want you to remember when it comes to faith and healing or praying for anything at all. Just because you have faith, it doesn't mean you have unlimited power. Faith is always an action that turns you back to God.

Faith doesn't give power. Faith is the ability to turn the whole situation over to God in prayer. Faith is saying, "Lord, I commit this person to your care because I know who you are. I ask that you heal and I have faith in you to decide!"

A quick word about miracles. There is a theological idea called "Common Grace." Common Grace describes those things God blesses us with everyday. Doctors, police officers and teachers are God's common grace to us. They are all blessed with gifts from God that help us. So the next time you have an illness and you pray for God to heal you, don't forget that the common grace of a doctor's prescription might be the way God chooses to work a miracle!

In your journal, write down some of the ways God has graced your life with "common grace." I think the things you find will surprise you!

A Walk on the Wild Side: Walking with the Master

My list of common grace experiences

My thoughts to the Master

Head over Heels for Jesus!

Scripture: Mark 9:30-50

Key Verse: Jesus called the Twelve and said, "If anyone wants to be first, he must be the very last, and the servant of all." *(Mark 9:35)*

About the Passage

Once again, Mark presents one of the core truths of the Gospel message: to be first, you have to be last. Did you notice the contrast between Jesus' words and the arguing of the disciples? Just after Jesus told them that he will die and rise again the disciples begin to argue over who is the greatest! I would like to think that I would be a more observant disciple (but I probably wouldn't be). Jesus responds to their childish antics by laying out the plain truth about following God. The last will be first and the first will be last.

Think about that for a second. What a ridiculous statement! No wonder the world thought Jesus was mad! Look at the world around you. Everything is about being first, about being the best, about succeeding, isn't it? But Jesus' way is about embracing the lowliest of all humans. In Jesus' day, children weren't even on the social ladder, never mind the bottom rung. So when Jesus instructs his disciples to open their arms to children, he is identifying himself with the least of all. Pretty simple!

"Causing others to sin" is a topic that is not so simple to explain. What we can say is, "keep the main thing, the main thing!" Christianity is about the grace and love of God in our lives and spreading that love to others. Don't confuse "children" (new Christians?) with a lot of rules and secret codes. Doing so would lead them down the wrong path.

The Application

Church denominations do many things differently. Some baptize babies, some adults; some dunk to baptize, some sprinkle water; some drink wine in communion, others have grape juice. The list goes on and on. What's most important is that we worship the same God and are striving to do his will. The differences are important to think and talk about but they pale in comparison to the message of the saving grace of Jesus Christ.

So don't put up walls between you and other Christians just because they do things differently. Christ came for all, not just for a few.

If there are Christians in your life that you have a tough time "living" with, stop and think. Spend your energy on spreading the gospel together instead of tearing each other apart.

My thoughts to the Master

"I Just Love You to Death!"

Scripture: Mark 10:1-16

Key Verse: For no one can lay any foundation other than the one already laid, which is Jesus Christ. *(1 Corinthians 3:11)*

About the Passage

I'm assuming that most of you are not married at this point, hopefully all of you! Nonetheless, this passage gives us a perfect opportunity to talk about relationships. The fact is that many of you will date during your teens. But interestingly, most of you will not marry the person you are dating now. Establishing a good foundation for all relationships is important. Here's what I'm getting at. Go back about 20 verses from the beginning of chapter 10 and you hear Jesus talk about his death. Go forward about 20 verses from the end of today's passage and you will hear Jesus talk about what?...you guessed it, his death. In the middle of talking about the sacrifice Christ is going to make, he talks about relationships between men and women. Even though the Pharisees want to trap Jesus by talking about divorce, he turns it around and focuses on marriage. He says that a good marriage has sacrifice at its foundation! As Christ died for us, a husband and wife should be ready to die for each other. Sounds pretty wild!

Jesus' words about children also relate to relationships. He "slaps the wrists" of the disciples for chasing the children away. Instead of looking down on them, they should be learning to come to him as the children do, in complete dependence. It is only when you have the attitude of a child that you will enter the Kingdom of God.

A Walk on the Wild Side: Walking with the Master

The Application

One note here: "casual" dating can be fun but I am going to talk about relationships that have gone into the "serious" stage. You can decide if your relationship is there yet or not!

Marriage is a serious thing. When I got married, one of my biggest adjustments was to remember to always think for two people. When I was single, I could make decisions for myself. But marriage means there is always another person to take into account, a person you should consider more important than yourself.

There are many reasons why marriages fail. Ultimately it comes down to not being willing to sacrifice for the other person. That's why I believe dating is a very important time in your life. Now, I'm not saying that you always have to think about marrying the person you are dating. What I am saying is that you shouldn't take your dating relationship lightly. Dating is a preparation time when you learn to put the other person before yourself. It is also a time when you learn what it means to love as Jesus loves. That is also the reason why dating a Christian is so important. Your relationship needs to be a place of mutual commitment and sacrifice that begins with an individual love for God. You see, it is only when we look to Christ's example that we can see how to truly love each other. This is a love that seems totally absurd to the world because it says, "I will show you my love by dying in your place!"

My thoughts to the Master

Giving 'til it Hurts!

Scripture: Mark 10:17-31

Key Verse: The disciples were even more amazed, and said to each other, "Who then can be saved?" Jesus looked at them and said, "With man this is impossible, but not with God; all things are possible with God." *(Mark 10:26-27)*

About the Passage

This is one of those passages that you read and say, "Ouch!" It really hits home, especially for us here in North America where we are all relatively wealthy (that is, relative to the rest of the world). It's not that we all have a lot of money or everything we want, but we are blessed with more than enough to get by. A few devos back, we talked about "mammon," which could be translated as money but it is actually more than that. It's our possessions, belongings or things we value.

The rich man came to Jesus asking for the way to eternal life. He knew all the commandments, all the rules and guidelines that he needed. He had even followed them "religiously" since he was young. But Jesus finds one thing he is missing. Is it the fact that he is wealthy? No, Jesus says to him, "There is something in your life that is more important than me—get rid of it!" And the man hangs his head and walks away. Sad. The disciples show a moment of brilliance and ask Jesus if this man can't be saved because of that one barrier, who can be saved? The message of this story is that there was nothing this man could do to earn eternal life. He could follow all the rules, be as nice as possible, do charity work but he could not save himself. It is only by turning our backs on everything and focusing only on Jesus that we find eternal life. "I am the way, the truth, and the life. No one comes to the Father except through me" (John 14:6). Turning your back on what the world offers may put you last in the eyes of the world, but in the Kingdom of God (which is where it really counts, by the way), you will be first!

The Application

I remember talking to a friend about Jesus and stuff. I asked him what was stopping him from even considering becoming a Christian. He said he didn't want to have to become a monk and go live in the desert, eating dust and drinking sand. I was kinda blown away by that response and asked him where he got that idea of Christianity. "Well," he said, "it always seems like Christians never have any fun and always have to be sullen and serious, thinking only of good things."

I think many of you will know people who think that way, or maybe even you think that way. There are two things I find very interesting about that response. First of all, my friend was definitely afraid of losing something. He didn't want to have to give up a lifestyle he enjoyed. Secondly, Christians need to stop worrying about what we're doing wrong and focus on the freedom Jesus gives us. If Christianity is just a set of rules, then it's no wonder people think we're always serious and sullen. Christianity isn't rules. Christianity is about looking toward the Master and realizing that, even though we have to give up something, we have gained EVERYTHING!! So, yeah, you're going to have to say "No" to some things in order to say "Yes" to Jesus. The value of what you gain is "60 billion" times greater than the price of the things you gave up! And with all your wealth, there is no price you could pay to earn the thing Christ gives you. He gave his life for you. Try giving him yours!

A Walk on the Wild Side: Walking with the Master

My thoughts to the Master

Simon Says...

Scripture: Mark 10:32-45

Key Verse: For even the Son of Man did not come to be served, but to serve, and to give his life as a ransom for many." *(Mark 10:45)*

About the Passage

Jesus must have been an amazingly patient person. Here he was with his disciples, sharing a very special moment as he talked about the reality of his death and resurrection. But the disciples, being the thoughtful people they were said, "Yeah, yeah Jesus, that's great, we want you to do whatever we want!" What? How would you have reacted to that statement if you were Jesus? Fortunately Jesus didn't give up and continued the conversation.

Jesus asked what it was they wanted from him. The incredible irony of this situation is that the disciples (James & John) had no idea what they were asking. Jesus went on and asked if they could "drink the cup that he drinks." It seemed that even after the third prediction of his death and resurrection, the disciples had no idea what he was really talking about. Not only did they misunderstand what Jesus said about himself, they also missed what he was saying about them. To "drink the cup" that Christ drinks meant that just as he would suffer and die, so his disciples would have to suffer and perhaps be killed.

That's a hard thing to hear. We know it and the disciples knew it. The disciples thought that following God would provide greatness and grandeur. That's why they asked the question they did. But instead, following God means you follow Christ's example. He came to be a servant and to give his life as the sacrifice for many. The problem is that this puts us in direct conflict with the world. Remember, those who are the greatest get to lord power over the "losers." But Christ says that if you want to be great, you need to be a slave to all. No wonder the world doesn't understand him! I just hope we do!

A Walk on the Wild Side: Walking with the Master

The Application

Can you imagine this conversation with a non-Christian. . .?

You: You should give Christ a chance and give your life to him.
Other: I hear that if I do, everything will be great in my life from there on in.
You: Well, actually not.
Other: Oh, so you mean that my life pretty much stays the same?
You: Well, actually not.
Other: So then what happens?
You: Well, chances are that you will have more trouble than you did before.
Other: I see. And so tell me again why I should be giving my life to him?

That really is a tough predicament, isn't it? To live the life that Christ calls us to means that we live exactly the opposite of how the world wants us to act. The world works towards greatness and self-gratification. The Christian works towards a life of service for the well being of others. The journey Christ asks us to walk is a wild one. But the reason we read this book (the Bible) is to see that Jesus does not just tell us how to live, but he shows us! And from his example, we can find out how to live as well!

My thoughts to the Master

Persistent Faith

Scripture: Mark 10:46-52

Key Verse: Now faith is being sure of what we hope for and certain of what we do not see. *(Hebrews 11:1)*

About the Passage

Some people sure have a lot of nerve! In the passage you just read, there are two groups of people that fit this category. There was the group that traveled with Jesus and tried to keep the blind man quiet. Isn't it interesting that the crowd thought they had "control" over Jesus? He was their miracle worker and no one was going to take him away from them! The crowd was less interested in what Jesus was saying and more intent on what he could do for them. Notice how beggars and "bottom-of-the-ladder" people were treated back then. Good thing that has changed today. . .right?

The other person with a lot of nerve is, of course, the beggar Bartimaeus (pronounced bart-e-may-us). He knew what he wanted—to see again. He also knew who could do it! There was nothing that was going to stop him from reaching his goal.

What a beautiful picture of persistent faith that is. When he finally met Jesus, there was no hesitation at all. He said, "My teacher, let me see again." There is something special about a persistent faith, one that doesn't give up, which keeps going no matter what obstacles get in the way. Neither the crowd, the social-ladder, nor the blindness could stop Bartimaeus from reaching that goal. Jesus honored the request of this man. But it is in the last sentence of this passage that we see what makes his faith real. "Immediately he received his sight and followed Jesus along the road." Bartimaeus knew who Jesus was and what he could do. He knew that his only response could be to follow Christ—and so he did.

The Application

Bartimaeus knew he had a problem; he was blind. He also knew that the only way to solve that problem was to get in contact with Jesus. Although there were obstacles along the way, he persisted and achieved his goal. The funny thing about this is that the disciples and the crowd around Jesus should have been doing the exact same thing. They too, were "blind" and needed Jesus to help them "see."

Today's story teaches us that part of faith is admitting that we have a problem. We could list specific issues but basically our problem is that we are human and screw up a lot. God has set out guidelines for how we should live. Take a look at the Ten Commandments (Exodus 2) or the Sermon on the Mount (Matthew 5). The standard is high and we often miss the mark. This is not a big surprise to God. He understands, so confess it to him.

After you have done that, call out to him, run up to him, push through the crowd to get to him and ask him to take control of your life. Jesus is willing and waiting to forgive. So here's what you do. On the journal page list all those things that are a problem for you. Then take them to God, asking him to take them from you. Then rip it out and throw it away because Christ has taken care of them!

My problems

My thoughts to the Master

Of Pomp and Circumstance?

Scripture: Mark 11:1-11

Key Verse: Those who went ahead and those who followed shouted, "Hosanna!" "Blessed is he who comes in the name of the Lord!" "Blessed is the coming kingdom of our father David!" "Hosanna in the highest!" (Mark 11:9-10)

About the Passage

Ah yes, Palm Sunday! A day of celebration and ceremony in the church. Little children coming down the aisles carrying palm branches and singing "Hosanna." Well, chances are that you won't be reading this on Palm Sunday. Chances are also that you may notice that there is no reference to palm branches in the passage you just read. You may also notice that, in Mark, there isn't even a donkey. So what's the big deal about this day anyway?

Here's another little Bible lesson for you. If you had a map and traced all the places Jesus has been over the last several chapters, you would see that he has been heading for Jerusalem—the symbolic center of "religion." Why did you think that throughout the gospel, Mark makes an effort to state where Jesus is (or maybe you didn't even notice!)? The disciples and followers thought this would be the time when Christ would bring in the Kingdom of God. Jesus would finally act! All of his followers were pumped about the future, knowing their King had finally arrived.

In contrast to that, in the many references to the excited crowd, nothing is said about Jesus. We don't know what he was doing, if he was smiling or laughing. He didn't join in the celebration but he also didn't stop it. Nothing is said. There is something significant about that nothing. Christ knew what he was riding into! He knew the pain, the humiliation and death that lay ahead. When Mark says "he looked around," I can almost see him standing there with a somber expression and letting out a big "sigh" in acknowledgement of the coming events. The crowd, on the other hand, sang and praised and shouted to the King. Were they right in doing so? I think so. Did they truly understand what kind of king he was? I don't think so.

The Application

Do you know the song "Refiner's Fire?" Probably. The words go like this. . . "Refiner's fire. My heart's one desire is to be holy. Set apart for you, Lord. I choose to be holy. Set apart for you my Master, ready to do your will." (Brian Derksen © 1990, Mercy Publishing)

It's one of my favorite songs. It is also a song that we shouldn't sing too often as far as I'm concerned. Read the words again. That's some pretty heavy-duty stuff we're singing. Do you think about it when you sing those words? Do you realize what you are singing? What does it mean to "choose to be holy?" That's making a big commitment. Ever thought of it that way?

One thing we can take out of today's passage is that it is great to sing and shout and praise God! After all, he deserves it. But it's also important to know what you are shouting about. The crowd going into Jerusalem was having a great time but didn't really understand what was going on. The challenge is to make sure you know what you're saying to God in the songs you sing. I would rather you make a decision not to sing "Refiner's Fire" because you're not ready to "choose to be holy" than to sing it simply because it makes you feel good. Think about it!

Here's what you do. Take a couple of your favorite worship songs, hymns or choruses, and write out the words in your journal. Then take some time to read them over and really understand what you are saying to God when you sing these songs. It is then up to you to decide if you are ready to make that kind of commitment to God.

A Walk on the Wild Side: Walking with the Master

My thoughts to the Master

Devotional #34: Figs Anyone?

Scripture: Mark 11:12-25

Key Verse: Remain in me, and I will remain in you. No branch can bear fruit by itself; it must remain in the vine. Neither can you bear fruit unless you remain in me. *(John 15:4)*

About the Passage

What is Jesus doing? The Bible really is a baffling book at times. Jesus curses a fig tree for not having figs on it when it was not the season for figs! It just doesn't seem to make much sense. It's like getting mad at a strawberry plant in winter because there are no strawberries on it! Was Jesus mad? Did he finally lose his "cool?" Maybe he wasn't a big fig fan?

We need to look at this in the context of the other passages around it. Remember, Jesus is heading into Jerusalem, the center of religion. He is also on his way to the Temple, God's house. Now, I don't think Jesus had anything personal against the fig tree, but he is hungry and there is no fruit on it to satisfy him. Likewise, Jerusalem is the place many people want to satisfy their spiritual hunger and from the outside, it looks promising. The Temple is there, Pharisees and other religious leaders are walking around. Generally, Jerusalem is looking very religious!

But Jesus knew that all the ceremony and outward appearances are nothing. They are like leaves on a fruitless tree. People who come to Jerusalem, looking to be fed, will walk away from it just as hungry as they were before. God was not being served in Jerusalem. People's lives are not showing the growth and fruit that comes from a dynamic relationship with God. As evidenced in the Temple, people are more interested in making money than in providing a place of prayer for people.

And so the next day, after they left Jerusalem, they saw the cursed fig tree withered. Without fruit, even the healthy outward appearances died.

A Walk on the Wild Side: Walking with the Master

The Application

I've decided to design a new bumper sticker. I'm not a bumper sticker fanatic, but I thought of a catchy saying that would probably sell. It would say, "You're following a fruitful fig tree!" Pretty good, eh! Now, the truth is that most people would have absolutely no idea what that is supposed to mean. But they would probably say something like "I'm following a fruit all right!"

If you want to be a fruitful fig tree there are some things that need to happen. First of all, you have to be rooted in the right place—you have to be a Christian. Before you even start thinking about bearing fruit, you need to be planted in the right soil. Second, you need to nurture your growth. This includes stuff like going to church, reading your Bible, praying, etc. Just doing all the right Christian "stuff" isn't enough. You might look good but there's no fruit. (Galatians 5:22-26). Third, you have to pay attention to what you hear and try to apply it to your life. Then when people come to you because you have the fruit they are hungry for, they are satisfied!

Work hard to turn what you hear in church, what you read in the Bible, into fruit. There are lots of people who are hungry for it! And besides, you get a free bumper sticker.

My thoughts to the Master

Mountainous Prayer!

Scripture: Mark 11:12-25

Key Verse: Therefore I tell you, whatever you ask for in prayer, believe that you have received it, and it will be yours. *(Mark 11:24)*

About the Passage

Yes, that is the same passage you read in the last devo (and if you didn't notice that, I'm a little concerned!). There's another aspect to this passage we must look at. Sometimes we read stuff in the Bible that I don't think we really believe. Take the last part of today's passage for example. Do you really believe that if you ask a mountain to jump into the lake, that it will? Have you ever tried it? Regardless, the point Jesus makes holds great truth.

Jesus is offering us another definition of faith. You see, faith is not just believing even though you doubt. The faith that Jesus is talking about here is faith that believes because there is absolutely, positively, definitely no doubt that God can do it! It's like a child bragging about their dad who can do anything in the world. In the same way, Jesus uses that ridiculous example of a mountain being thrown into the sea to show that God can do it; all we need to do is ask. Jesus not only proves to the disciples that God is big and strong, he is telling them to never let a prayer go unanswered because no one bothered asking him for it!

Jesus is also talking about forgiving others. Just as a doubting heart can be a hindrance, so can a heart that is not willing to forgive. It's back to the fig tree again (devo #34). We can't pray to God and say how much we love him and how much faith we have in him without being willing to extend that love to others through forgiveness. Jesus reminds us that the Christian life is not just about you (singular) and God. It's about you (plural) and him!

The Application

There are or will be times in life when you pray to God very specifically. You may pray about the health of a family member, asking that God will heal them. Other times you may pray about a trip or the safety of a child. In those cases we pray not "your will be done" but "please let it turn out this way." And you know what, that's good! Far too often we pray around issues, not wanting to offend God with our direct requests. We need to let God know what is on our minds and what we would like to see.

But as Jesus warns, these things need to be done in complete, undoubting faith. When I asked God to take the cancer out of my mom's body I did so because I knew he could! If I knew the doctor could have healed my mom completely, I would have gone up to him and asked him to do it—I would have begged him to do it. I wouldn't have said, "Well, whatever you do is fine with me!"

We need to have faith that God is in control and is making a decision that works out for good somewhere along the line. Does that mean you won't perhaps be saddened or emotionally affected by the decision? No way! But our faith in God is something that says, "Lord, there's this mountain in front of me and I can't move it but I know you can. So please move it! And if you don't move it, show me another way around it." Mountainous prayer lets us take the problems in life and offer them back to God knowing that he will carry us through it.

A Walk on the Wild Side: Walking with the Master 111

My thoughts to the Master

I'm Not Telling!

Scripture: Mark 11:27-33

Key Verse: "See, I will send my messenger, who will prepare the way before me. Then suddenly the Lord you are seeking will come to his temple; the messenger of the covenant, whom you desire, will come," says the LORD Almighty. *(Malachi 3:1)*

About the Passage

Whenever I read this passage, I imagine an argument between two kids. I picture one standing on the porch and the other at the end of the sidewalk. The kid on the porch is yelling, "I'm not telling, I'm not telling" while the other is stomping her feet, yelling at the top of her voice. This whole passage is like that kind of immature argument.

Remember that Jesus has just cleaned out the Temple and the religious "big guns" wondered who gave him permission? Jesus responds with a question of his own (he always seems to do that— it would get pretty annoying). The religious leaders huddle and discuss how they should answer this question. They soon realize they are trapped and so plead ignorance. In response, Jesus says, "Well, then I'm not going to tell you either."

There are two basic reasons for Jesus' response. First of all, Jesus remains quiet because the evidence has been all around them all along. It started with John the Baptist and the Pharisees didn't believe him. It continued with Jesus' teachings, signs, wonders, miracles but those didn't seem to convince them either. So why would they believe Jesus now? Mark goes a long way to show us who Jesus is, through Jesus' actions and testimony.

The second reason is found in the huddled conversation between the leaders. From the decision they made, it is clear they were not interested in the truth. They were worried about what the people would think of them and wanted to keep the people on their side. Jesus knew his words meant very little to the religious leaders of the day.

A Walk on the Wild Side: Walking with the Master

The Application

Image this. . . There is a group of people engaged in conversation. You walk up to them and ask, "what are you guys talking about?" They respond with, "nothing." How would that make you feel? Does it make you wonder if they were talking about one of your faults? Now if you are, for instance, walking into the room with toilet paper hanging out of your pants, I think you can be sure they ARE talking about you.

Sometimes I wonder if Jesus treats us the same way. Not that he ignores us but I wonder why he doesn't answer us when we ask him who he is. Often we come to God saying, "Show me you are real!" and, at times, there is no answer. We wonder why. At the same time, God may be wondering why we ask in the first place. Are we blind that we can't see the beautiful creation all around us? Are we illiterate and unable to find God in the Scriptures? Are we so deaf we can't hear the experiences of people around us who have "seen" God working in their lives? This isn't to say that God won't work in your life in supernatural ways. God is telling you about himself 24 hours a day. Take some time to reflect and journal about the ways God can/is telling you about himself.

My thoughts to the Master

Devotional #37: Responding to Grace

Scripture: Mark 12:1-12

Key Verse: For it is by grace you have been saved, through faith—and this not from yourselves, it is the gift of God—not by works, so that no one can boast. *(Ephesians 2:8-9)*

About the Passage

This harsh parable cuts straight to the heart of the matter. Basically, it says this. God has entrusted a particular task to the religious leaders (Pharisees, Sadducees, etc.). They are to raise, grow and nurture fruitful people (remember the fig tree?). They have been given the responsibility of providing people with the information, direction and encouragement they need to become strong followers of God. But there is a problem. They begin seeing God's work as their own. Eventually, they want the vineyard for themselves. After all, they were the ones who worked it. So God sent in prophets and other messengers to help them understand but they were treated cruelly and even killed.

The real story here is not so much about the selfish cruelty of the religious leaders. The story is about their response to grace. You see, God offers them another option. Despite all they have done, he says, "I will send my Son and they will certainly respect him." He gives them another chance. He offers them grace. Rather than seeing this as an opportunity to make past wrongs right, the leaders see the son as the final barrier to be crossed. They think the vineyard will certainly be theirs after the son is dead. And so they kill him and throw his body out of the vineyard. The irony is that these leaders will eventually be thrown out themselves. They felt they didn't need the owner—God. They had the gifts and talent to run the vineyard on their own but they forgot an important principle—they didn't own the vineyard in the first place. God gave them the responsibility and talents to be leaders. It was only through grace that they were in the positions they were. Reject that grace and you reject everything that goes with it!

The Application

Tell me if you see anything wrong with this picture (A parable by Dave). . .

You are writing a math test. The problem is you forgot to study because you were busy doing other important things like playing Nintendo 64. You get to class and try to explain the situation to your teacher. She nods understandingly and says, "Well, how about I give you the answer sheet to work off of?" Sounds good! You sit down and start working. You hand in the test and next class find out you failed the test! The teacher comes up to you and asks how that could happen since you had the answer sheet. You explain that you did the first couple of questions with the sheet but found it so easy you decided to do it on your own. The teacher is disappointed but says you can rewrite the test with the answer sheet again, if you like. But that will mean you wouldn't get to your friend's house for the 24-Hour-Nintendo-64-a-thon. So you say thanks but no; you'll stick with the F.

Sounds wacko, doesn't it?! But the truth is we do that a lot with God. He offers us the answer key, the Bible, and he gives us all the talent and abilities we need to live successfully. But too often we say "no thanks" and try to do it on our own. Our response to his grace needs to be "Yes God, I'll take it! And I'll use it for what you want as well!" Remember, as Christians, it's God's Kingdom we're building, not our own!

My thoughts to the Master

Giving to the Giver

Scripture: Mark 12:13-17

Key Verse: Then Jesus said to them, "Give to Caesar what is Caesar's and to God what is God's." And they were amazed at him. (Mark 12:17)

About the Passage

"Ah ha!" the religious leaders exclaim. They have set the trap to catch Jesus no matter which way he answers. But these guys are not quite as smart as they think they are. Let me spell out the scenario for you. The question of taxes is a huge one. Land is a major identifying mark for any nation. The Romans, led by Caesar, had come and taken "God's" land away from the people of Judea (Israel). If Jesus says that they should pay taxes to Caesar, he is going against culture and the people will be very upset with him. On the other hand, if he says you should not be paying taxes to Caesar, you can be sure the religious leaders will go right over to the Roman governor and tattle on Jesus. He will be guilty of tax evasion! So apparently, he is trapped.

Well, Jesus gets to the heart of the matter. He flips over a Roman coin with Caesar's imprint and states, "Give to Caesar what belongs to him and give to God what is his." In an instant the events of the past days spring to mind—the cleansing of the Temple (Mark 11:15-19), the withered fig tree (11:12-14, 20-21) and the parable of the vineyard (11:27-23). Was God really getting what belonged to him? The religious leaders have corrupted the Temple, practiced fruitless religion, rejected God's messengers, and planned to kill his Son. They have become so concerned about all the rules, regulations, laws and appearances that they have forgotten to give God what is his. These religious leaders pay taxes to Caesar but don't give God his due!

A Walk on the Wild Side: Walking with the Master

The Application

Now we need to ask, "what does it mean to give God what is his?" Hmmm, good question. Here's a simple answer. God has given each of us gifts and talents and abilities. Read Romans 12 and you will see a number of examples listed there. Some are teachers, some are prophets, some are leaders, etc. Each person has a part to play in the big picture. When we talk about giving God what is his, we are saying, you need to make sure you are using those gifts to serve God somehow. After all, they are his and he's just loaning them to you for a while.

Think of it this way, the taxes you pay (or most likely, your parents pay) are an investment. They go to help keep the roads smooth, provide police and fire services, help the public and private schools run, and a lot of other stuff. As a taxpayer, you (or again, probably your parents) have the right to ask the government, "am I getting my money's worth?" If the roads aren't smooth, you have the right to ask "why not?" After all, it is your money.

In the same way, God has made an investment in us. He has put a lot of work into not only saving us from our sins (see John 3:16) but also in blessing us with gifts and abilities. He did it for a reason. He wants us to build his Kingdom, tell others about him, serve in the church and help other people out. If we are not doing those things, God has the right to ask us, "am I getting my money's worth?" In what ways has God gifted you? How can you use these gifts? Take some time to answer those questions in your journal.

My thoughts to the Master

Clutter!

Scripture: Mark 12:18-27

Key Verse: He is not the God of the dead, but of the living. You are badly mistaken!" *(Mark 12:27)*

About the Passage

Well, it now appears that this "battle" between the religious leaders and Jesus is getting downright nasty! It is interesting to see how the fights get more and more intense as we get closer and closer to the cross.

The Sadducees were a group of religious leaders kind of like the Pharisees. There were differences between them but they both represented the "religious establishment." As Mark points out to us, the Sadducees did not believe in resurrection. In fact, they did not believe in any kind of after life at all—once you're dead, you're dead! That information sheds a different light on the question they are asking Jesus. We quickly realize that they were not asking a serious question at all. Rather, they were mocking Christ and the idea of heaven and resurrection altogether. They were interested in making the idea of resurrection look ridiculous.

Jesus' answer puts them in their place. He knew the Sadducees had a lot of ideas about many things (I know that's vague but bear with me!). He also knew that they didn't know the Scriptures as well as they said they did and that they didn't have any clue about the true power of God. They were so preoccupied with all this "religious clutter" that they missed the whole point of being children of God. They felt it was more important to argue than it was to be in God's Word, actively searching for truth. They had God boxed in so tightly it was almost as if he was no more powerful than you and me!

The Application

"Clutter" is a part of everyday life. There is another name for clutter these days and it's called "the Internet." Now don't get me wrong. I have spent some time surfing the Web, looking for helpful bits of info and cool web sites. But, when it comes right down to it, all this information is simply clutter in my mind. It doesn't help me live any better. It doesn't make me any smarter (expect maybe at Trivial Pursuit). All it really does is fill space in my brain.

The same can be true of our Christian walk. There is a lot of stuff we can fill our minds with that may be interesting or make us look knowledgeable, but really, it doesn't help us live successful Christian lives. That's part of what Jesus was hammering the Sadducees for. They had lots of stuff in their head, but if they would have known the Scriptures like they said they did, they would have realized that most of that stuff was simply clutter. Modern day denominations tend to get caught up in that as well. There are differences between all the denominations but if those differences become the all-consuming focus, then they are nothing but clutter—stuff that takes up space. The bottom line is this, things we clutter our minds with, such as which way to baptize, when will Jesus return?, where do dinosaurs fit into the creation story?, were those six actual days in the creation story?, can never become more important than the core of the gospel message. So here's what you do: in the journal area write down in as few words as possible what you believe the "core" or the most important thing about Christianity is. Then what you do is take some time and figure out if that is what is occupying your mind. If you find your mind filled with "clutter," think about, pray about, talk about ways that you can get your life focused on the core.

The most important thing about Christianity

My thoughts to the Master

J.O.Y.

Scripture: Mark 12:28-34

Key Verse: "The most important one," answered Jesus, "is this: 'Hear, O Israel, the Lord our God, the Lord is one. Love the Lord your God with all your heart and with all your soul and with all your mind and with all your strength.' The second is this: 'Love your neighbor as yourself.' There is no commandment greater than these." (Mark 12:29-31)

About the Passage

Yesterday I left you to think about what is core and do some journaling about it. The beautiful thing about the Bible is that, if you dedicate yourself to reading it, you will find out what is most important about being a Christian. Today's passage is a perfect example of that.

On the one hand, there were the Sadducees who asked Jesus about "clutter"—things that didn't make much difference in the Kingdom of God. On the other hand, you just read about another teacher of the law who asked Jesus a sincere question about the greatest commandment. Read the beginning of the passage again and you will see that these are not two separate instances. This teacher of the law heard the argument going on between Jesus and the Sadducees and noticed Jesus' wise answer. It was almost like this teacher was saying, "That's a good answer Rabbi. But if all that stuff is clutter, then what is the most important thing about a life with God? What is the core of the issue?"

Jesus' answer was simple. He said we should love God with everything we have and love our neighbor as we would love ourselves. You see, the second part of that commandment is not a simple "love others the way you would like to be loved" but is, treat others the same way you treat yourself (does the "Golden Rule" ring a bell?). That's it! It's that simple! Well, saying it is simple; living it is perhaps not quite so easy.

The Application

As a young lad, I was taught a simple and effective way to remember how Christians are supposed to live. It was called "the J.O.Y. principle" and worked something like this. If you want to have JOY in your life, then you need to get your priorities straight. The first priority is JESUS (notice it starts with "J"). The second is OTHERS (take note of the "O"). And the third priority is YOURSELF (you guessed it, "Y"). If you live life this way, you will have JOY! Well, it may seem a little childish to you to think that way but hey, I remember it 20 years later!

Take a minute to look back to yesterday's journaling and read what you described as the "core" of being Christian. Now think about the words of Jesus from today's passage. Do these two match up? If it is necessary, improve your list of core Christian values. Use today's passage as a reference and put it in your own words.

Like I said before, the core message is really quite simple but living it out can be difficult. Once you have your core statement ready, write down some ways you can live this practically, from day to day. Compare notes with a friend or talk to your parents or pastor about it.

You will continue to mess up and not always live up to the standard, but if you take time to think and concentrate on it, you will, as Jesus said, "not be far from the kingdom of God."

A Walk on the Wild Side: Walking with the Master

Practical ways to live the "main" thing

My thoughts to the Master

"That's All I Got!"

Scripture: Mark 12:35-44

Key Verse: For you know the grace of our Lord Jesus Christ, that though he was rich, yet for your sakes he became poor, so that you through his poverty might become rich. *(2 Corinthians 8:9)*

About the Passage

If you had to come up with one theme that ties together the three "stories" in this passage, what would it be? Seriously, read through the passage again and see what you can come up with. These three scenes help answer the question "Who is Jesus and what kind of ruler is he anyway?"

The first scene describes stuff about David. Jesus is saying he is not the same kind of king as David. David was a mighty warrior, an army general and a defeater of nations. Jesus is not that. Our question, however, is still not answered.

The second scene is about Jesus' denouncement (or "hammering") of the teachers of the law. They walk around looking for praise and attention, but their practices are evil and anything but godly. They are more concerned with looking good than doing good. Jesus is not like that. But what is Jesus like?

The third scene is at the Temple. Jesus is watching people give money to the treasury. Rich people come by and give lots of money—which is good. Jesus doesn't condemn what they are doing. Then a widow comes by and drops in two copper coins. It is everything she has to live on. Jesus calls the disciples over and draws their attention to the widow and her offering. The irony is that Jesus answers the question we asked before. What kind of king is Jesus? He is the one who gives everything he has to the Kingdom of God.

The Application

The story is told of a TV preacher who promised to pray for people if they would trace their hand on a piece of paper, write their prayer requests on the paper hand and mail it off to him (with a check to support the ministry). The preacher's office was flooded with prayer requests (and checks). The preacher's staff quickly responded by ripping open the envelopes, depositing the checks and throwing the prayer requests into the dumpster out back and that is exactly where a TV crew found them. The prayer hands were never even touched.

Gets you pretty angry doesn't it!? Jesus has some harsh words for people who know all the right words to say but live complete lies. You see, Jesus' words are not only descriptive of who he is but also of who we are to be. He doesn't want fakers in his kingdom. He doesn't want you to play games. He doesn't want you to act like you believe all this stuff if you don't! Knowing the right words to say and being able to pray long and hard in public doesn't make you Christian. What makes you Christian is taking all you have and using it in the Kingdom of God. Go back and read Mark 8:34-37. Tell me, what good does it do for that TV preacher to have all that money when he dies? Nothing! Jesus says we need to be like the widow and give everything we have. That's pretty wild! Take some time to talk to God about the things that are stopping you from giving everything to him. Go ahead, he's listening!

My thoughts to the Master

Watch!

Scripture: Mark 13:1-37

Key Verse: "Therefore keep watch because you do not know when the owner of the house will come back— whether in the evening, or at midnight, or when the rooster crows, or at dawn." *(Mark 13:35)*

About the Passage

The question I am going to ask you right off the bat is this: did you actually read that whole passage? If not, go back and read it. I'm serious, go do it now! I won't go on until you get back. This is a pretty overwhelming passage of Scripture and so it is important that we give it attention.

Here's a little role-playing for you to do. Pretend you are one of the first readers of Mark's gospel. It has been 20-30 years since Jesus ascended into heaven and you are sitting in a room with a group of other people, anxiously waiting for the manuscript (document, letter) to be read for the first time. You hear all the familiar stories that have been passed down from generation to generation and you dream of actually being there with Jesus. Then the leader gets to the passage that you just read today (they didn't have chapters on the original) and you hear all the horrible things that will happen to God's followers before the return of Christ. You shudder inwardly and think to yourself, "Yes, the end is near. These are exactly the things that are happening to us."

The fact is that the predictions Jesus makes were happening to the first Christians reading Mark's gospel, and they are still happening today. The first readers, second readers, third readers, and so on, all believed that they were in the last days before Christ's return, (just as many believe that today). The key to this entire passage is the last word—Watch! You see, Jesus makes it very clear that no one, except the Father, knows when the end will come. So don't worry about when it happens, but be ready and be hopeful because it will happen. Jesus is telling his disciples to live faithfully and work diligently because he is not here now but will be coming back!

A Walk on the Wild Side: Walking with the Master

The Application

It is easy to get caught up in looking for signs and indicators that will tell us when the end of the world is coming. There are people who dedicate their entire ministry to figuring out when the day of Christ's return will be, based on the events that are happening around the world. But Jesus is saying that the events and disasters that happen globally are not the things we should focus on. We should be focusing our attention on the fact that he is returning. And that is good news and bad news.

Here is the bad news. Because of our confession that Christ is Lord, the world will make things difficult for us. There will be persecution, arrests, betrayal and death. Now, I have to say that it is hard for us in North America to understand these words. We live in relative peace and harmony with society around us. People may bug us because we are Christians but we certainly are not being thrown into jail for confessing Christ. What Jesus is saying is that the "wild" gospel is something that will put us in direct conflict with what the world believes and that will stir things up!

The good news is that we have very little to worry about. Whatever situation we get into, God will provide his Spirit to deal with the situation. All we need to do is live faithfully, watching for his return!

My thoughts to the Master

Uncommon Love

Scripture: Mark 14:1-11

Key Verse: If I give all I possess to the poor and surrender my body to the flames, but have not love, I gain nothing. *(1 Corinthians 13:3)*

About the Passage

How much do you love Jesus? Some people answer that question before we have a chance to ask it. Take the woman in today's passage for example. She was an unknown person (we never do find out her name) who comes into the place where Jesus is visiting and pours a jar of perfume on Jesus' feet. The jar was worth a year's wages! That's pretty wild. Let's not even start talking about the way that room must have smelled for the next month or so!

The really interesting part of this story is the reaction of the people sitting with Christ. You may expect them to object to this use of perfume and say, "Hey, that's really going to stink things up in here!" or "Now what is she going to use for herself?" But instead, they give a pretty logical response, don't they? "[That perfume] could have been sold for more than a year's wages and the money given to the poor." Nothing wrong with that response.

However, Jesus said her actions were good and beautiful. He explained that he would not always be with them and since he would soon be gone, the celebration of his presence made sense. This woman has simply expressed her love for Jesus in a beautiful, yet uncommon way. She demonstrated how our love for Christ is what is important and not necessarily our devotion to religious ritual.

The other aspect of this story is the continued preparation for the death of Christ on the cross. Pouring perfume on a body was commonly done to combat the odors that came from the decaying corpse. This woman showed her love to Jesus in response to the love he would show for her and all others on the cross.

The Application

How much do you love Jesus? What are the ways you express that love to him? The woman in today's story illustrates an important principle—how we spend time, money, and energy will very often determine where our love lies. It is easy to see that in North America we are in love with "stuff." We have lots of material goods and we just seem to need more and more. People spend hundreds of thousands of dollars on things that are geared to entertainment. Would you be willing to spend a year's worth of allowance on Jesus to show him how much you love him? The wild thing about the story is that we never find out the woman's name. We hear only about her act of love. So all the money she spent on perfume did not get her name in lights or even get her a "nice person" medal. But it did glorify Christ and for her, that was worth it!

How do you express your love for Christ? Do you feel comfortable raising your hands in worship, falling to your knees in prayer or closing your eyes during a song? We don't need to worry about what others will say and just do it! After all, Jesus' ultimate expression of love to us was beyond wild. In your journal, take a minute to write down different ways you can show Christ how much you love him.

Ways I can show Christ how much I love him.

My thoughts to the Master

"Surely Not I?"

Scripture: Mark 14:10-26

Key Verse: Even my close friend, whom I trusted, he who shared my bread, has lifted up his heel against me. *(Psalm 41:9)*

About the Passage

Whenever I read this passage, I think of a James Bond movie where 007 is rendezvousing with another agent who is wearing a red flower and will answer only to the code words, "the chocolate mousse is always in season!" The disciples are told to look for a man carrying a water jug and tell him that the Master wants a place to celebrate Passover. Mark goes into great detail explaining the circumstances and events surrounding the death of Christ. The reason he does that is this—there is nothing accidental about the death of Jesus. He wants to make sure we know that this is what God wanted to happen and that Jesus was obedient in following that plan. Jesus is in control of the situation, he knows what is going to happen in order for God's plan to be fulfilled.

The contrast in this passage is in the disobedience of Judas. We knew (since 3:19, in fact) that he would be the one to betray Jesus. Isn't it interesting that Judas' act, which was not a very nice thing to do, is all part of God's plan? God took the disobedience of Judas, and turned it into something good. That really makes me think about the way God works!

The response of the disciples to Jesus' words that someone in that room would betray him is interesting. Each one asks "It's not me, is it Jesus?" as if they are unsure. We can imagine how their minds are racing and questioning their loyalty to "the Christ."

The Application

This passage raises some tough questions in my mind. I am always surprised at the response of the disciples to Jesus' statement that someone would betray him. I would like to think that if Jesus said that kind of thing to me, I would be asking myself, "Well, I know it isn't me, so I wonder who it is?"

The thing we cannot escape is that all of us are responsible in some way for putting Jesus on the cross. It isn't like God's plan was going great until Judas came along and messed things up for him. Judas was part of the plan, an unfortunate player in it, but part of it nonetheless.

We are all naturally sinful. Remember that passage from Romans 3:23, "For all have sinned and fall short of the glory of God." Jesus went to the cross not just because Judas betrayed him, not because the plan failed somehow, not because he got tired of fighting with the leaders all the time but because he loves us so much he wants to take that sin out of our lives and give us a fresh start. We all had a part in putting Jesus on the cross, not just the people in 33 A.D. (approximate date of Jesus' death). We also got a second chance because of the love shown to us on the cross. All we need to do is accept it. And if you haven't yet, I think it would be a good thing to do! Talk to someone you trust about taking that step!

A Walk on the Wild Side: Walking with the Master

My thoughts to the Master

This is My Body...My Blood

Scripture: Mark 14:12-26

Key Verse: Is not the cup of thanksgiving for which we give thanks a participation in the blood of Christ? And is not the bread that we break a participation in the body of Christ? *(1 Corinthians 10:16)*

About the Passage

There is something very significant about the Lord's Supper. It has to do with the Passover, the Jewish celebration that was happening exactly at this time.

Here's a quick Bible history lesson (you can read Exodus 12 as well). You may remember that the Passover originated in Egypt. The people of Israel had been slaves there for hundreds of years and God, through Moses, was preparing to lead them out. Pharaoh, on the other hand, had a different idea. So God sent plagues through the land with the last one being the death of every firstborn offspring as the angel of death passed through. God instructed the Israelites to perform some very specific acts, which included painting the blood of a lamb on their doorposts so the angel of death would "pass-over" their home (hence the name!). That was what finally got them out of Egypt. So Passover was a huge celebration of the freedom God gave to the Israelites.

Are you seeing the connection here? It is fitting that during this celebration of freedom, Christ prepares himself and his disciples for the ultimate freedom-giving act, his death on the cross. Just as the blood of a lamb saved the Israelites in Egypt, so does Christ's blood save the disciples and us now.

A Walk on the Wild Side: Walking with the Master

The Application

When I was growing up, I used to dread communion services at church. There was the option for people who were not taking it to leave the sanctuary and wait in the lobby. But my parents would never let me do that! They would make me stay in the sanctuary while they got to have bread and grape juice. And then people would pray afterwards and we had to stand. They prayed so long that I felt like I would fall over! It was very traumatic.

I am now older and a bit wiser, and I have come to understand what taking the Lord's Supper means for us as Christians. It is a very important thing. When I take it, I am remembering the very act that gave me life, Christ's death on the cross. When you read through the Apostle Paul's writings, you see that he takes communion very seriously and even says that if there is some stuff in your life that needs cleaning up, do that before you take communion. The freedom that we are given through Christ is nothing to take lightly!

The other significant thing about communion is the fact that we take it together with other believers. Taking the bread and the cup identifies us with Jesus. It signifies that "we have decided to follow in Christ's steps, even if that means suffering as he did." People who have made the same commitment surround us and so we are not alone in our journey. That's perhaps the greatest thing about this walk on the wild side, the fact that we are not walking it by ourselves but are with others who have the same goal we do!

My thoughts to the Master

Devotional #46

Faithful One

Scripture: Mark 14:27-52

Key Verse: All this is from God, who reconciled us to himself through Christ and gave us the ministry of reconciliation: that God was reconciling the world to himself in Christ, not counting men's sins against them. And he has committed to us the message of reconciliation.
(2 Corinthians 5:18-19)

About The Passage

I will be honest with you and say that we will not be dealing a lot with that naked guy running through the garden. However, he, along with the disciples, along with Judas, brings up an important aspect of Jesus' last days. That can be summed up in one word "Abandonment." You will quickly notice that Jesus' closest followers are leaving en masse (means in a big group kinda thing). From predictions of Peter's denial, to falling asleep in the garden, to a "friendly" kiss, to running away without any underwear on, the disciples are abandoning Jesus as he gets closer to the cross. It seems that his words, "Whoever loses his life for me and for the gospel will save it" (8:35b) did not sink in all that deeply.

The contrast in all this is Jesus. Amidst the unfaithfulness or unreliability of the disciples, Jesus is praying to God with a deeply troubled heart. We really get a good look at Jesus' humanity. He asks God for some other way for this plan to be accomplished. But he also prays, "If there isn't any other way out of this, then I will do what you want me to." He knows the pain and torture that await him and he, just like any human being, would love to avoid that pain. But he also knows the reason for it all. He understands that there is something much bigger here then his own comfort. Christ is faithful, for our sake, even when the cost is high. He is faithful not only in that he will carry through with the plan, but he will carry through despite the mistakes, cowardliness and abandonment of all those around. Thanks be to God for that!

The Application

I'm not sure if you've noticed or not, but Mark always give us two ways of looking at and learning from a passage. This one is no exception. For me, the garden of Gethsemane is a frightening place. What if Jesus decided not to go through with it all? What if he decided to disobey the Father and find his own course in life? When he says to Peter "the spirit is willing but the body is weak" I believe he is saying that to himself just as much as to the others.

One way we can look at this passage is through the disciples' eyes. Once again, they messed up. Through falling asleep, outright betrayal and running away under pressure, they have abandoned Jesus. The question we ask is, "Do I do that sometimes? When Jesus asks me to do something, do I leave him, taking the easy way out?" Somehow the name Jonah sounds familiar here! Don't be too quick to judge the disciples without looking at your life first.

The second way is to look at Jesus under pressure. We look at the disciples and can say, "that is how we are." But when we look at Jesus, we should be saying, "that is how we should be!" Jesus knew there was great risk and cost in doing what he did but he also knew that it was God's will—and so he did it! Are there situations in your life that will be painful to do but you know will lead to good in the end? Take some time to write those things in your journal and then pray about them. Ask for the courage and strength to respond like Jesus did to those "challenging" situations.

My thoughts to the Master

Devotional #47

Guilty As Charged?

Scripture: Mark 14:53-72

Key Verse: O God, whom I praise, do not remain silent, for wicked and deceitful men have opened their mouths against me; they have spoken against me with lying tongues. *(Psalm 109:1-2)*

About The Passage

You will notice something very interesting about the way Mark has written this Gospel. The first part of the book goes by very quickly. Jesus is moving here and there, doing this and that, teaching those people and these people. The last few chapters of Mark move very slowly. In fact, from the entry into Jerusalem onward, everything is taken day by day. In the first part of the book, Mark tells the stories of Jesus teaching his disciples and us how to live. In the last part, leading up to the crucifixion, Jesus lives out those teachings. The key verse to remember for today's passage is once again Mark 8:35 "For whoever wants to save his life will lose it, but whoever loses his life for me and for the gospel will save it."

Jesus says very little in the trial. He knows that the testimony brought before him is false (although, isn't it funny that even the false witnesses proclaim the truth!), so why try and defend against them. However, the one thing he does say is the one thing that will ultimately condemn him to death. "Are you the Christ, the Son of the Blessed One?" he is asked. Jesus responds, "I am." There are many different things he could have said instead of that. He could have weaseled his way out of it saying, "Well, actually I'm the son of Mary. Honest, ask her!" But he stood up for the truth even though that condemned him to the terrible events that lay ahead.

On the other hand, we have Peter. He was asked basically the same kind of questions. He, too, knew which answers were the "right" ones and which would get him into trouble. He chose to save his own life. You notice that once the crowd heard his answers they left him alone. But it was deep within himself that he knew that in trying to save his own life, he lost something much more valuable.

A Walk on the Wild Side: Walking with the Master

The Application

Have you ever been asked the type of questions Peter was asked? Have you ever had someone come up to you and ask if you are a Christian? I have. It's a very scary thing! Reading through Christian history, you will quickly see that Christians have been asked this question for centuries. In times when being a Christian was cause for being killed, authorities would ask you to do one simple thing and you could go free. All you had to say was that you were not a follower of Jesus Christ. That simple statement would free you from being fed to the lions or burned at the stake.

It's hard to know what we would choose. I believe it is something we need to be prepared to answer. It's kinda an old "cliché-ish" saying but if being Christian was a crime and you were asked if you were one, would you be guilty? You would avoid a lot of problems by saying "No" because not only would people not bug you about being a Christian but you also wouldn't have to worry about what you say, what you do, where you go, etc. But what does that do to your relationship with God? Some people may pay more attention to you and you may become more popular, but is "saving your life" now worth losing what you could have later? Follow the example of Jesus who boldly faced the consequences of being on God's side!

My thoughts to the Master

The Games We Play

Scripture: Mark 15:1-20

Key Verse: He was oppressed and afflicted, yet he did not open his mouth; he was led like a lamb to the slaughter, and as a sheep before her shearers is silent, so he did not open his mouth. *(Isaiah 53:7)*

About The Passage

It's interesting to watch Jesus in action. He doesn't say much. He doesn't defend himself against the accusations of others. He simply stands there, silently. Yet, as you read these passages, you can't help but feel that he is in control here. He has an authority that even Pilate senses as he stands amazed in front of him. The silence of Jesus throughout the trials and beatings is significant. It points to the peace God provides to those who do his will.

The interesting thing about this passage is the way Mark gives us a "behind-the-scenes" look at the goings on. We know, for instance, that much of the testimony brought against Jesus was a lie. We also know that Pilate, who believed that Jesus should go free, condemned him simply to keep the crowds happy. And we know that the religious leaders were handing out flyers, pamphlets or something to stir up the crowd against Jesus. The "power" they had over the situation came from dirty, backhanded tricks and schemes. The release of Barabbas rather than Jesus is significant as well. When the people thought of the Messiah, they believed it was someone who would ride into town with "guns a-blazing," taking out the Roman rulers. When Jesus proved not to be this type of person, they decided to get someone whom they knew would do all he could to free Israel— Barabbas. His methods did not matter as long as he accomplished what they wanted. Again, it is a sad commentary on "the crowd" who, even after all of Jesus' teachings, seem to be more interested in themselves than in the truth!

The Application

There is a lot of stuff in this passage we could talk about. I'll point out one aspect. "Playing games" is a popular thing in religion today. We sometimes talk about "church politics." Or the "religious right" that exists in the United States, which is a group of Christians who get involved in political policies and agendas. These are all things we, as Christians, do to enforce what we believe to be true and right. Are these things bad? No, they can be helpful in promoting Christian values. But they can become destructive when we compromise what we know to be right for what we would like to see happen (and those aren't always the same thing)! That was true in today's passage. Pilate knew Jesus was innocent but he played the game the religious leaders wanted him to play. The coaxing of the religious leaders easily swayed the crowd who had followed Jesus and cheered when he entered Jerusalem. In all of this, I feel for the religious leaders who simply wanted to get rid of Jesus because they were jealous of him. I think that sometimes, we do the same thing. Sometimes we try to get out of something or we try to get into something and we use our "religiousness" as an excuse. Have you ever heard, "I don't feel God has called me to do that."? Or my favorite, "I believe God has called me to plant a church in the Bahamas!"

Whatever you do, don't play games with your faith! Let the Truth be the Truth whatever the consequences. Look at the example of Jesus again. He knew what the truth would do to him but he also knew the peace that God gives to those who serve him faithfully!

My thoughts to the Master

The Main Thing

Devotional #49

Scripture: Mark 15:21-47

Key Verse: And they crucified him. Dividing up his clothes, they cast lots to see what each would get. *(Mark 15:24)*

About the Passage

You need to realize something about the Christian faith; it is the crucifixion alone that makes Christianity seem ridiculous to many people. There is nothing pleasant about the cross. We tend to make it look pretty and shiny with smooth edges and nicely stained. Crucifixion was used to kill barbarians and evil people who committed great wrongs in society. It was such a terrible form of execution that Roman citizens often refused to talk about it. In fact, entire armies could be persuaded to turn around and retreat at the threat of crucifixion for those who were captured. There is something very offensive about the cross!

And so when we read Mark's brief narrative on the crucifixion of Jesus, it's no wonder he uses very few words to describe what went on. "And they crucified him" was all he said. He didn't have to say anything more because this is the event he talked about all along! The suffering, the losing of one's life, the beatings, the true definition of Messiah, all point to the cross. What makes this event even worse is that Jesus is alone. Even his Father has forsaken him. The only people present are those who are insulting and mocking him as they walk by. Isn't it interesting that throughout the entire Gospel, people (disciples included) have difficulty seeing and understanding who Jesus really is. Yet, when he is on the cross as an innocent man, when his "mission" is brought to completion, when all the words he said about the Temple and suffering are seen on the cross, then he is recognized for who he is. "Surely, this man was the Son of God!"

A Walk on the Wild Side: Walking with the Master

The Application

I had a college professor who made a comment that has stayed with me to this day. We were studying the gospels and came to this exact time in Jesus' life. He stopped in the middle of a sentence, turned around and looked at the class. He said, "Don't you ever forget that none of this is possible without the death of Jesus of Nazareth. Don't ever skip over the cross!" He's right! We do tend to leave the cross alone. As evangelical Christians, we tend to leap right over the cross and go straight to the resurrection. We want to celebrate and be happy, not face the gruesome cross that looms before us.

Friends, don't ever forget that Jesus died for you! We often say Jesus died for us but somehow we think that he just kinda transported himself to a different dimension and then came out of the grave three days later. No! Jesus of Nazareth died on that cross! His heart stopped pumping, his brain stopped sending signals to the rest of his body, his lungs stopped taking in oxygen. He was dead—because of me, because of you!

This is the main thing of Christianity. We were the ones who should have been up there on the cross but instead, Jesus went there for us. He wasn't an evil person; he didn't commit some great crime that earned him this treatment. There was nothing legitimate about his condemnation or his trial other than the fact that God wanted it to happen because he loves us so much! Take some time to talk to God, thanking him for this. Write your prayers in your journal.

My thoughts to the Master

Just the Beginning

Scripture: Mark 16: 1-8

Key Verse: "Don't be alarmed," he said. "You are looking for Jesus the Nazarene, who was crucified. He has risen! He is not here. See the place where they laid him." *(Mark 16:6)*

About the Passage

What's happened here? You may have noticed that your Bible still has about ten verses left to Mark. Well, so does mine. However, those are not the words that Mark wrote; they were added later by a scribe or some other editor. Mark meant for his gospel to end at verse eight. "But why?" you ask. Good question. I am not saying that verses 9-20 are in any way not part of Scripture. They do contain "good words" for us to hear. But if we want to experience the full impact of Mark's Gospel, then we need to concentrate on why he ended it like he did.

The women, who were faithful enough to be at the cross with Jesus (if at a distance), go to the tomb to anoint the dead body, as is the custom. There they find the stone already rolled away and the body of Jesus gone. A mysterious man is sitting in the tomb and tells them to go tell the disciples that Jesus is alive, as he said, and they should go meet him in Galilee.

The women, full of excitement and anticipation to see Jesus again, rush off to tell the disciples. They go with the disciples to Galilee and have a big "welcome back" party, right!? Wrong!

Rather, the women, trembling and bewildered, run off and never tell anyone because they are afraid! What kind of ending is that? No wonder somebody felt they needed to add something else to that story. Did the disciples ever see Jesus again? Was Jesus waiting around in Galilee for them to show up and finally he just went back into heaven? What about the Great Commission and stuff like that? By ending the gospel this way, Mark is asking us a question. "You know the good news, you know that Jesus rose from the dead, so what are you going to do with it? Are you going to hide in a corner and not tell anyone, or will you go out and proclaim it to everyone?" The choice, as Mark puts it, is up to you!

The Application

Have you ever read those Choose Your Own Adventure books? They are the ones where you are presented with a scenario and then asked to decide what you are going to do. If you choose to run, turn to page 12. If you choose to eat the moldy VegiBurger, turn to page 53. They really are a lot of fun.

We have come to the end of the Gospel of Mark and it is now that you need to choose which way you are going to walk. If you read through the whole thing (and not just skipped to the end) you will have been presented with many different ways to change your life; many different paths you can take that allow you to walk with the Master. You need to decide what you are going to do with all of this. Is it going to make a difference in your life? Is knowing how Jesus' disciples responded to so many of Jesus' words and works going to make you more sensitive to Christ's working in your life? Is knowing that you can come to God with anything, even asking him to toss this mountain into the sea, going to change the way you pray? Is knowing the way God forgives even though we continually "miss the point" going to help you take more risks in living your Christian life? Is knowing that God calls you to give everything to him going to help you order your priorities from day to day?

The ball is in your court now. God has spoken to you through the book of Mark and he wants to know how you are going to respond. Why don't you talk to him about that right now? God Bless You!

A Walk on the Wild Side: Walking with the Master

My thoughts to the Master